Advance Praise for *The Secret Life of Communication*

I found *The Secret Life of Communication* clear, insightful, and touching. It is obvious that Dr. Wilson has a passion for helping human beings communicate from a place of love and deep respect.

Gay Hendricks, PhD
Author, *The Big Leap*
Coauthor, with Dr. Kathlyn Hendricks, of *Conscious Loving*

Most of us know that good communication is key to successful relationships at home and at work. But did you know that communicating well with others begins by honest communication with yourself? In *The Secret Life of Communication*, Annie Wilson will show you the connection between your inner feelings and beliefs and how you relate to others around you. This book is full of "aha" moments.

Ken Blanchard, PhD
Coauthor of *The One Minute Manager*® and *Great Leaders Grow*

Dr. Annie B. Wilson is opening the door for people to discover the possibility of true oneness and love in their communications with others. This wonderful book teaches us about the transformation that occurs through four different types of communication between people, based on the inner experience of consciousness that one carries.

In the first stage, we are separate and communicate from our own self's needs with little understanding of others. Later we move into a deeper sense of respect and honoring of others and communicate with desire for us all to get our needs met; however, we still experience ourselves as separate.

However, in the final stage, as we experience a state of Unity within ourselves, we experience the depth and beauty of real communication that stems from our experience of love within. Now all communication is about the expression of Love and the experience of beauty and peace that can occur between two people.

Dr. Annie B. shares her own experience of this final level as she experienced Unity and the expression of consciousness that flows from that state, free from what the world thinks she should be. Here communication flows naturally from the source of one's being where love is the only criteria for being together.

This depth of communication is something that we should all strive for in our relationships so that we can know real peace between people. For those people who are seeking to know true communication that expresses the Oneness and Unity of our being, this book will guide you toward that reality within yourself.

Dr. (Ibrahim) R. Jaffe, MD
Murshid Murrabai Ruhi, Shadhiliyya Sufi Order, USA
President, University of Spiritual Healing and Sufism
Founder, Shadhiliyya Sufi Center, USA
Director, DrJaffeMD.com

The Secret Life of
COMMUNICATION
Opening to Unlimited Love

ANNIE B. WILSON, PhD

iUniverse, Inc.
Bloomington

The Secret Life of Communication
Opening to Unlimited Love

iUniverse books may be ordered through booksellers or by contacting:

iUniverse
1663 Liberty Drive
Bloomington, IN 47403
www.iuniverse.com
1-800-Authors (1-800-288-4677)

ISBN: 978-1-4759-4614-7 (sc)
ISBN: 978-1-4759-4616-1 (hc)
ISBN: 978-1-4759-4615-4 (e)

Library of Congress Control Number: 2012915153

Printed in the United States of America

iUniverse rev. date: 09/07/2012

To every person
who is enough,
right now.
(Psst ~ that's you!)

Contents

Foreword

What keeps any of us from living fully within our truest nature or spiritual self? What blocks us from witnessing ourselves as loving and compassionate people who want to succeed and not fail? The block is a common question that lies at the heart of most of our fear and pain: *Am I worthy of being loved, powerful, and beautiful?* I am not talking about outer beauty, but rather an inner beauty that makes all humans special in their own right.

At the heart of our very existence lies a strange phenomenon of wanting what shows up around us, while at the same time being terrified of being controlled by it. We want it, but we fear it. By "it," I am referring to our need to be loved and seen at the deepest level.

Thus, the question to ask is this: *Is it possible to be strong and vulnerable?* Is it possible to be strong and vulnerable within the confines of human engagement, without being guarded, defensive, or, worse, spiritually dim? Yes, it is!

Beyond the boundaries of our professional and personal identification lies a place where our spirits run free, without fear of retribution. It is within this space where we communicate from an unlimited source of love and certainty. We might call this boundless energy and truth our spiritual heart.

Here is where I believe this book, *The Secret Life of Communication*, stands alone in its ability to reach the masses. There are few manuscripts that speak so honestly and directly about human discourse from a heart-centered approach. The genuine and, at times, raw depiction of the author's own journey of self-exploration through the four layers of communication is exactly what is needed to have a deeper understanding of what it means to live and communicate from our hearts. When we operate from this place of boundless joy and connection, we find our true nature and then live abundantly.

From the day I met her, Annie Barron Wilson, affectionately known as Dr. Annie B., has never wavered in her desire to fully know herself. She has consistently reached into her soul to find meaning, not only in times of great hardship and pain, but also during times of great success and prominence. It has been her ultimate dream to fulfill her life purpose of helping others to know themselves.

In meeting her, you would find her spirit to be akin to the hummingbird. This beautiful creature is known in the Andes of South America as the bird that opens the heart. When the hurt that caused us to close our hearts gets a chance to heal, our hearts are free to open again. It is through Dr. Annie B.'s presence that her readers will experience their hearts awakening once more.

Annie is a true teacher and modern-day mystic. She radiates a beautiful balance of strength and sensitivity required to move and touch people's lives in the deepest way. When Annie began her own path of investigating the varying intricacies of human communication, she started with herself. She plunged headfirst into her own power center—her heart—and confronted her own pictures and beliefs of unworthiness. While transforming these attitudes, she discovered it was possible to change and to change at the deepest level—spiritually.

The Secret Life of Communication is not only a wonderful guide for those looking to find their inner voice and truth, but also a tremendous instrument for deepening one's connection to the divine. Even the title of this book implies there are more discoveries to be made about the heart's magnetism and role in revealing our own divine nature.

In sparkling and delightful prose, Annie draws her readers inward so they can distinguish their own mirror reflections from what is illusion in a safe and nonthreatening manner. She also does a remarkable job of teaching the daily practice of *Remembrance* along with illustrating practical methods for self-care, which ultimately transforms all those who are curious and brave enough to step into their own hearts. I invite you to punch your ticket with enthusiasm and take the clandestine route to inner freedom ... for this book will *not* disappoint.

Rebecca Lynn Hamm, MA, LPC
Cofounder of The One Center of Austin

Introduction

When I was fifteen, the highlight of my day was coming home from school to snuggle with my baby sister, Bridget. I'd drop my backpack at the door and head straight for Bridget's room to kiss her cheeks and wake her up from her nap. As I cradled Bridget in my arms, her sweet baby smell and the weight of her body relaxing onto my chest always calmed my nerves and lifted my spirits. One day, instead of finding her soundly sleeping, I ran into Bridget's room to find her screaming as if someone were torturing her.

When I got to her crib, I noticed that she was asleep, even though she was crying so loudly. Right away I could see what was causing Bridget's pain. Her little fingers were completely entwined in her hair, and she was pulling as hard as she could. The sound of her cries told me that she felt not only pain, but also fear. Without waking her, I gently released her grip and caressed her sweet little head. Immediately, she relaxed and heaved a big sigh as she continued to sleep.

Sometimes, I'm just like Bridget. I cause my own pain but don't realize it. I think I'm trapped by someone else's words or actions, and I can't see a way out. Have you ever felt like that? We can choose to sleep through life to find some measure of relief from the constant chatter in our minds that tells us nothing will ever get better. That chatter is wrong! It *can* get better, if we are willing to pay attention to the full spectrum of our internal communication, not just the chatter in our heads.

That's what *The Secret Life of Communication* is about—how to listen and respond to all aspects of communication so that we can build healthy relationships and open up to the unlimited love that exists in each and every moment. It is possible, and you are worthy of experiencing it.

Life's challenges can diminish our awareness
of the communication occurring in
our bodies, hearts, and spirits.

That's what happened to me. Over time, I grew from a sensitive, intuitive, creative child into a well-educated, analytical adult who gave all of her attention to thoughts, words, and actions. My focus was turned outside of myself because I was a pleaser and a doer. I looked to others to validate my worth.

Throughout my teens and twenties, I lived in fear of rejection. Even though friends admired me, employers awarded my performance, and an Ivy League school accepted me into its master's program, it was not enough to make me feel secure. My opinion of myself remained poor, regardless of how others saw me. Isn't that odd?

I looked to others to assess my worth
and then rejected their opinion when it was positive.

When I reached my early thirties, I had earned a master's degree in management from Cornell University's Hotel School and was building a career I enjoyed. However, my quality of life suffered from a relentless drive to achieve goals and please people.

I attracted bosses and romantic partners who increased my pain rather than enhancing my enjoyment of life. In 2003, I decided to pursue my doctorate degree because I assumed that another advanced degree would lead to a job that would make me happy.

My communication remained firmly rooted in
thoughts, words, and actions.
I ignored my intuition, my emotions, and my body sensations
because I did not trust them.

My assumption about graduate school was partially correct: it did lead to my happiness, but not because of a job. I chose to study at the University of Texas at Austin after meeting Oscar Mink, a professor in the education college who looked like Santa Claus and exuded love. At first when I talked with him, I did not think of him as exuding love, but I noticed that being in his presence felt like a warm embrace. I looked forward to his classes and usually arrived early and stayed late.

Sometimes I made appointments with Oscar simply to talk about what I was reading or thinking about; I wanted to be near him and listen to his stories. One day, I walked into Oscar's office when he was meeting with another student. Oscar pointed at me, smiling, and said to his student, "I always know when someone is going to change the world." I thought to myself, *Could he really mean me?*

*For the first time in my adult life, I felt tingles run up my spine
and imagined my chest bursting with light.
Because I trusted Oscar, I also trusted
my body's response to his words.*

Oscar's perception of me matched my secret wish: to change the world by increasing hope. During my PhD program, I researched hope in the workplace, focusing on teachers and nurses. At the same time, I dove headfirst into the deep end of a pool of personal healing.

*I realized that I had to help myself
before I could help others.*

In addition to participating in personal development workshops and meeting with a counselor, I attended the University of Spiritual Healing and Sufism, where I restored my relationship with my body, heart, and spirit. In 2007, I completed my PhD and accepted a position as Director of Organizational Development with Providence Health and Services in Missoula, Montana.

I enjoyed providing leadership development and staff training to employees throughout western Montana. Very quickly, however, I noticed that the standardized curriculum was not making much of a difference. Managers continued coming to me with the same questions: How can I stop my employees from bickering with one another? How can I help my employees deal with stress and constant change? Why did I ever agree to be a manager?

My approach to helping the managers answer their questions was to guide them below the surface of words and actions, to the deeper layers of communication. They were astonished, and I was pleased, when after just one custom workshop or a couple of personal coaching sessions, employees resolved long-standing grievances.

Patient satisfaction improved, and employees collaborated more often.

Eventually, our chief medical officer asked me to help physicians with their communication skills. This was an invitation I had been waiting for! Conflict between physicians and nurses had become a hot topic in medical literature as well as management meetings, and many good people, all of whom wanted to heal patients, were suffering.

Because I held deep respect for all who worked with patients (and because I knew no single group of employees—like doctors—was responsible for the communication breakdowns), I approached my coaching sessions with an open heart and mind. In response, the physicians opened their minds and hearts. They became willing and able to build new communication skills, which enabled them to lower their stress, further improve patient outcomes, and experience deeper satisfaction.

After five years, I resigned from my position in order to move back to Austin and build my own business, helping people from all industries and all walks of life to develop healthy communication as they remember that they are enough, right now.

In this book, I will share with you
the same principles that I teach my clients.

In my coaching sessions, webinars, and workshops, I discuss common topics like how to resolve conflict, how to build healthy relationships, and how to manage change. My approach is particularly effective because I also discuss the internal elements of communication—the *sources* of conflict, collaboration, and business outcomes.

If you think of communication as a tree, the first three chapters of this book describe the roots. As you read, you'll learn about your own standard equipment (your mind, body, heart, and spirit/intuition) and how each piece contributes to communication. You'll also learn to recognize life as a mirror of your beliefs about your own worthiness and "enoughness."

The next seven chapters are the trunk, branches, and leaves of our tree. In them, I will describe what happens when we communicate from each of the four layers of communication.

I will show you how to recognize what's really going on in communication
and how to move into the deeper layers,
where communication becomes
productive, enjoyable, even healing.

In each chapter, you will find stories from my own journey and those of my clients, to add humor and clarity along the way. While every story is true, I have changed names and minor details to protect my clients' privacy and anonymity. Let's begin!

What Happens When We Communicate?

If you've ever taken a seminar about effective communication, you probably learned that less than 10 percent of the effect of communication can be attributed to words. The rest is attributed to tone of voice and nonverbal cues. Why is that? Why can't we just say what we want to say and expect the other person to understand us? Because communication is all about interpretation—what goes on inside of us when we listen to or watch someone else communicate.

Have you ever noticed how much communication occurs in your own head?

I often have conversations with my friends without their participation! I think about talking with them, imagine their responses, and then, because my thoughts are so vivid, sometimes can't remember if the conversation actually happened. We don't just communicate with our voices (or hands) and body language. Those are important because they help us to express ourselves to others. But before we ever communicate with another person, we communicate with ourselves! We do it while others are speaking, too.

Our bodies, minds, hearts, and spirits
are always communicating within us.

Think of little Bridget. When her fingers were entwined in her hair, her body was communicating, *I'm in pain!* Because she didn't know how to free herself, her survival instinct probably was thinking, *I'm trapped!* And from the sound of her cries, I could tell that her heart was feeling scared. All of that communication was occurring in a nine-month-old baby, just as it occurs within each of us in every moment.

The next time you feel trapped by someone else's actions or words,
try to notice what's going through your mind,
how your emotional heart is feeling,
and what it feels like to be in your body.

10

That's what I did one summer when my neighbor was driving me crazy. For years, I had wanted to live in an old, craftsman-style home, so it was a joyful moment when I signed the lease for the little, blue 1930s cottage with a view of the river and bright red tulips growing in its flowerbeds. After having lived in an apartment I hated for twelve months, I felt happy to be in a house again, especially one with so much charm. What could be wrong with that? Plenty!

The old wood floors creaked more than I expected, and there was a tenant in the basement. During my first few weeks in the house, I felt terrible about walking around in the morning, knowing that my neighbor might be woken up by my movements. While I did everything I could think of not to disturb her, she slammed her door every time she went in or out, and she blasted her music, even at night when I was trying to rest.

Because I had moved from a much larger apartment, I needed storage space in the little garage that came with the house. For weeks, I asked my neighbor to move some of her things to make room for me. Eventually, she gave me less than half the amount of space I had requested, but I made do.

Are you starting to see a difference between my neighbor and me? On the surface, it might seem that I was more considerate than she was. That might be, but ...

If I had invested my energy in criticizing her,
blaming her for my discomfort or otherwise focusing on her,
I would have missed the point.

I had something to learn from this situation, something about how I was communicating with myself. Instead of dwelling on how my neighbor should change, I decided to look at what part I was playing in my own discomfort.

Every time I felt annoyed by my neighbor's behavior, I asked myself, *What is my irritation really about?* Then I paused for a few seconds to notice whatever came to my mind. At first, I wasn't sure how to interpret the thoughts and images that came to my mind after asking the question, but after about a week, I figured it out: my neighbor was very comfortable taking up space.

She did not apologize for being who she was. Apparently, she did not care if she disturbed other people, as long as she honored what felt good to her in the moment. Wow! *What would it feel like to live that way?* I wondered. All my life, I had tried to make other people comfortable, even at the expense of my own comfort. Also, when I anticipated success, the idea of taking up lots of space (by being energetically "big") was overwhelming. Sometimes I felt guilty at the thought of it.

*In my mind, I held an assumption that
it was not okay for me to take up space,
and if I couldn't take up space,
then my neighbor shouldn't either!*

That's what my irritation was really about: she got to do something that I was denied. When I recognized this difference between my neighbor and me, I decided to challenge my long-held belief that it was not okay for me to take up space. I slammed my door a couple of times, not to disturb my neighbor or to spite her, but simply to see what it would feel like. I have to admit, it felt good! And the world did not come to an end. Nobody yelled at me or told me to be quiet. In fact, nothing happened at all.

After that revelation, I decided not to feel guilty for walking around in the morning. This might sound crazy, but for the first few days, I had to tell myself that I was not doing anything wrong when I took an extra trip to the kitchen (and over my neighbor's bedroom) for tea. During the first two weeks of this experiment, I awoke feeling very anxious nearly every day. My breathing was shallow, my stomach felt nauseous, and my mind raced with frantic thoughts that didn't make much sense.

Previously, when I would awaken feeling anxious, I would quickly get out of bed and distract myself with some activity or television. This time, I decided to make room for my anxiety, to be with it instead of trying to pretend it didn't exist. Before getting out of bed, I paused, gave attention to my breathing, and slowly expanded each breath.

It felt awkward to breathe deeply, taking up more physical space and more oxygen, but I did it anyway because I wanted to break the cycle of anxiety. As I gently expanded each breath, I repeated to myself, *There is enough space for everyone, including me.* The first few times I said that to myself, I wondered, *Is that really true?*

In the past, I would have asked that question and then become distracted by memories of the many times I was told to be quiet or not attract attention while I was growing up. I would have let those memories tell me what was true, that I should not take up space. This time, I watched the memories float through my mind and noticed my body feeling more anxious; then I decided to think of the memories as a movie, separate from me and my truth. As soon as I made that decision, the memories seemed to lose their grip on my attention, and I was able to notice my own inner voice.

I asked myself, *Is it really true that there is enough space for everyone, including me?* In my mind's eye, I saw the word *Yes* written in a lovely black script, with terra cotta and gold colors swirling behind it. It was beautiful.

When I gave my attention to the word and the beauty surrounding it, the anxiety in my body released. My stomach and shoulders relaxed. I felt my body sink into the bed as my breath naturally expanded. I even felt a little excited, as if I had just opened a present.

My heart, spirit, and body knew it was true:
there was enough space for me.

However, my mind struggled a bit. This new experience did not seem logical. It did not match the messages I had paid attention to for decades, the ones that told me there was not enough space for me, and I should not disturb or inconvenience anyone. I accepted that struggle, because I knew that my mind took care of me by deciding what was true, based on repetition.

I decided to be gentle with my mind by not judging it for believing something about me that was not true and that had caused me a lot of pain over the years. Instead, I just decided to repeat the process of asking myself if there was enough space for me, and then pausing to breathe fully and pay attention to my internal response, until my mind caught up.

I could have avoided all that reflection and confronted my neighbor instead. I didn't do that for two reasons. First, she got louder when I asked her to be quiet. Second, and more importantly, I knew that ...

*My power expanded when I paid attention to
the communication going on inside myself first,
before speaking to someone else about his or her behavior.*

When I paid attention to my thoughts, emotions, body sensations, and intuition, new possibilities came into view. In the end, my neighbor served as a mirror so I could recognize and free myself from the illusion that I was less worthy of taking up space. That was much more satisfying than a confrontation would have been.

Life Is a Mirror of What We Believe about Ourselves

What would you say if I told you that everything in life is a mirror of what you believe about yourself? When I teach this concept in workshops, some people take offense because they assume that I mean they are responsible for everyone and everything in their lives (which is definitely not true). Other people ask me, "Annie, I'm my own person. How can someone else be a mirror of my beliefs about myself?"

In reply, I explain that our perception of ourselves, other people, and the events we experience or observe is shaped by our beliefs about ourselves. In this chapter, I will show you how this works and how looking into the mirror can increase your joy and freedom.

Many spiritual traditions and motivational speakers teach that life is a mirror of our thoughts or emotions. I teach that life mirrors our deep beliefs about ourselves because it is those beliefs that *create* thoughts and emotions.

When we identify and transform painful beliefs
like "I am not enough," thoughts and emotions shift on their own,
and we become more open to love.

For example, I have an optimistic nature and am very sensitive to hearing people complain or gripe. For years, whenever a coworker or friend griped about something, I became very irritated. I usually didn't say anything to them, but in my mind, I spent a lot of time and energy criticizing them and thinking about why they should not complain. When I heard them, my shoulders became tense, and sometimes my fists clenched, and I got a stomachache.

In one way, those people were a mirror for me because their verbal griping was a reflection of my silent but fierce criticism. I could have looked at this situation and determined that I should just stop criticizing other people if I wanted the reflection to change, but if I had stopped there, I would have missed the deeper lesson.

Life's deeper reflections are subtle, not literal.

When I looked beyond the surface and asked myself what my irritation was really about, eventually I realized that it annoyed me to hear others say what they thought or felt while I censored myself in an attempt to be a "good girl." I believed that I had to be positive and agreeable at all times in order for people to like me.

To shift what I saw in the mirror
(other people complaining around me),
I needed to believe that it was okay for me to be honest about
how I really felt and what I thought.

I did not have to actually express those feelings or thoughts to anyone. I just had to believe that it would be okay if I did, that I had permission to be honest and open without fearing that people would reject me and I would be left alone.

That example was a bit serious, but looking into life's mirror can be playful too. Have you ever seen Wendy's *Where's the Beef?* commercial? It was one of the most popular commercials of 1984 and starred a short, elderly lady who demanded to know, "Where's the beef?" as she peered over the counter of a burger joint whose burgers had huge buns with little burgers. (If you haven't seen it, a quick Internet search will bring up the video.)

What was that commercial trying to get us to do? Buy hamburgers. Why would we buy hamburgers if we had lots of chicken in our refrigerators? That commercial's purpose was to let us know that beef was more valuable, and we didn't have enough of it.

That's what commercials do; they reinforce our sense of lack so that we will consume. It is very effective because thoughts that we are not enough or there is not enough for us are familiar to most of us. *Oh, I don't have enough beef. I'd better go to Wendy's!*

That was a very successful campaign for Wendy's, and it was a funny commercial, but the subliminal message was: *You don't have enough beef, and you won't feel satisfied until you get some from Wendy's.* That commercial capitalized on the common belief: *I don't have enough.*

*Everything we pay attention to
either confirms or contradicts
our core beliefs about ourselves.*

Many of us use television to escape painful thoughts only to find them growing stronger in the background. That's what happened to me. I have never been a person who could watch one or two shows and then turn my TV off. If I was home, my TV was on. I didn't particularly like watching TV, but it helped to distract me from loneliness and worry … or so I thought.

In 2005, I decided to conduct an experiment. I wanted to find out how watching television affected my communication, especially my communication with myself. For two weeks, before turning on the TV, I noticed my emotions, how my body felt, my anxiety level, and the thoughts that were going through my mind. Then, I watched a show that I typically enjoyed and noticed how I felt afterward. Each time, after just fifteen minutes of watching, I noticed that my breathing had become shallow, my stomach and shoulders had become tight, and I felt more anxious or irritable.

Even though I was watching shows about home improvement and nature, I found my thoughts about myself becoming very negative. I noticed myself thinking things like, *I should have a house like that at this stage in my life ... My home isn't nice enough ... I'm not thin enough ... I should go on a diet ... I'm hungry! ... I'm lonely ... Too bad no one will want to be with me because I'm too fat, and my home isn't nice enough.* You get the picture, right?

These statements were reinforcing the core belief: I am not enough.

I noticed my reactions early on in my experiment, but I continued it for the full two weeks because I was hoping the first few days had been a fluke. I didn't want to give up my TV. I negotiated with myself that it might not be so bad if I watched less TV, so I turned off my TV and covered it with a blanket to prevent myself from watching more than two shows.

I drew red stop signs and taped them to the TV screen. I turned the TV around. Each tactic worked for oh, about an hour. After two weeks, it was clear that my habit of using the TV to distract myself was not doing me any good, and moderation was not an option. I decided I had to take a drastic step if I was going to save myself from this self-destructive habit.

I threw my TV into a Dumpster. It wasn't environmentally friendly of me, but it sure felt good! My TV was the style with a built-in VHS player, so it was heavy. Late one evening, I lugged it down the stairs from my apartment, across the sea of anthills that stood in place of a lawn, to the Dumpster.

I grabbed the TV from its built-in carrying lip, swung, and tossed it—right into the side of the Dumpster. With a resounding crash, it landed on the concrete, clinging to life. For a split second, I thought, *Maybe it's salvageable!* Then, *No! This is what I want!* I picked up the television for the last time, aimed at the open door, and heaved it in.

What do you think happened next? Did I suddenly feel wonderful about myself and realize the truth—that I was enough? No.

Television had not created the belief that I was not enough;
it had reinforced it by mirroring back to me
the negative thoughts I already held.

Changing the belief that I am not enough is a journey, one that I am glad to be on every day because my life keeps getting better and more fun. Now, when I watch for them, I receive lessons and reminders in unexpected, even silly ways.

One summer shortly after finishing my graduate studies, I moved to Missoula, Montana, which had a population of around 80,000 people. After having lived in Austin, Texas, for six years, I was glad to be in a city with a slower pace. However, I soon realized that although everything on the outside had slowed down, my pace on the inside was still racing. That's because …

No matter what others told me,
I always believed I wasn't doing enough.

On a beautiful Saturday morning three weeks into my life as a Missoulian, I decided to get a latte on my way to explore a nearby hiking trail. A coworker had recommended a local espresso shop, and although I knew I was driving in the right direction, I was not sure where to turn.

For some reason, that morning I had awoken feeling a bit anxious and tired. I was driving on one of Missoula's few busy streets and had to make a quick decision. I turned left and immediately knew that I had turned too early. As I sped toward the first parking lot I could find, I had to slam on my brakes to avoid hitting an elderly lady who was crossing the driveway.

While she slowly walked by, I smiled and thought to myself, *Good for her. She's out and about with her walker, and isn't that a sweet hat she's wearing?* When the woman had passed by, I quickly turned around and reentered the busy street. I turned left at the next intersection, only to find that I had made the same mistake—I had turned too soon. By this point, I was getting angry.

*The anxiety I had woken up with
had turned into impatience.*

Just as before, I whipped into the nearest parking lot, only to find that same elderly lady walking across the driveway! Don't ask me how she'd gotten there before me, but she had. This time, I did not appreciate her hat.

I impatiently waited for her to cross, and then I sped into the parking lot with the intention of driving through it to the other side, where I could see my destination. Imagine my surprise when I realized I couldn't drive through that parking lot. I had to turn around—again! With an impatient huff, I jerked my car into reverse, cranked the steering wheel, and started to turn around. Then, I noticed it.

Right in front of my nose was a parked truck displaying a bumper sticker that read, "Did you move here to be in a hurry?" I saw that question and laughed, answering out loud, "No, I did not move here to be in a hurry!"

That bumper sticker broke through my anxiety and impatience. It served as a mirror, helping me to pause and remember how I wanted to engage with life. I slowly completed my turn around in the parking lot, reentered the busy street, and arrived at the espresso shop relaxed and ready to enjoy the rest of the day (I ordered decaf!).

Life is a mirror of our core beliefs about ourselves. Sometimes the reflection is obvious, while other times it is subtle and easy to miss.

When we listen only to our thoughts,
we are likely to miss the subtle cues that life offers to us.

That's why in the next chapter we will explore in detail what I call the organs of perception: the mind, body, heart, and spirit/intuition. When we pay attention to the communication coming from all of these "organs," it is much easier to recognize and open up to love in every moment.

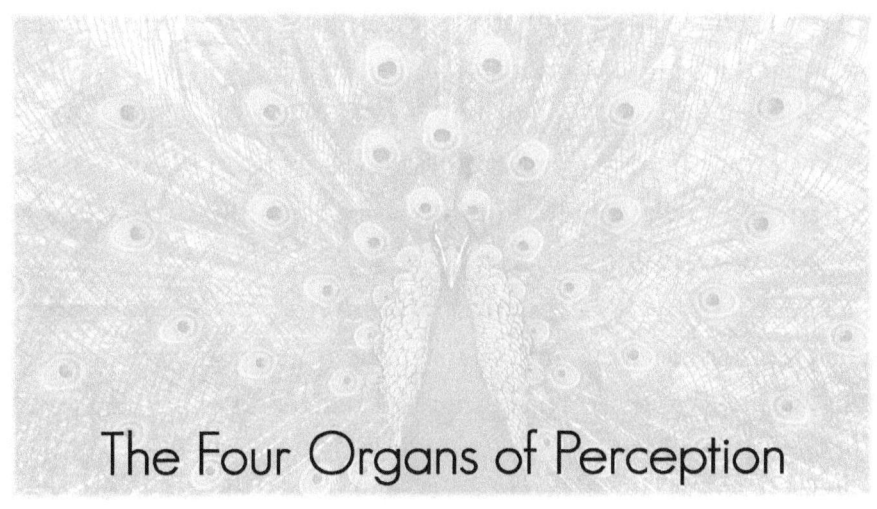

The Four Organs of Perception

Have you ever heard the phrase "Perception is reality"? It's true! Words are just the tip of the iceberg when it comes to communication. Our perception, or what we pay attention to, affects how we interpret words, body sensations, body language, and tone of voice, and that interpretation creates our reality.

In this chapter, I will describe what I call the organs of perception: the mind, body, heart, and spirit/intuition, and I will explain how they can contribute to communication. Please keep in mind that there is no real separation among your mind, body, heart, and spirit. I'll describe them one at a time, simply to make it easier to recognize how each one functions.

The Mind Is Beautiful and Limited

In many modern cultures, thinking is highly valued, and minds are well developed. Even so, brain studies have shown that an average person consciously notices only one out of every million sensory events.[1] One out of every million! That means we are missing a lot of information.

This might surprise you, but the mind is much more than a resource for acquiring information and making decisions. We actually have three types of brain, which you might also think of as three different minds.[2]

Most of us think of the conscious mind, the neocortical brain, when we talk about the mind. That area of the brain is responsible for conscious thought, reasoning, language, and planning.

For some, life experiences and formal education have reinforced a reliance on the neocortical brain and its rational, logical thought processes, investing much time and energy in deciding, *This means that … That happened because,* or, *This is good, and that is bad.* Such reasoning certainly is useful, but …

In order for our conscious minds to thrive,
they have to communicate with the other two areas of the brain,
what I call the emotional mind and the mind of survival.

The middle part of the brain, the limbic brain, is responsible for processing memories and emotions. This emotional mind helps us perceive intimacy within relationships, which is very important because most of us have a strong need to feel like we belong. Even though emotions are processed in this part of the brain, I will delve into them in my discussion of the heart.

The mind of survival, what scientists refer to as the primitive or reptilian brain, enhances our survival by making sure we eat, sleep, store information, and respond to threat. It also is responsible for body sensations, which I will describe in my discussion of the body.

The mind of survival helps us keep ourselves safe. It prompts babies to cry when they're hungry and adults to fight, flee, or freeze when they feel threatened.

*Our survival response is designed to elicit
a strong reaction that passes quickly.*

This mind of survival is an excellent resource when we allow it to do its work and then move on, like when a hungry baby stops crying and relaxes into her mother's arms in response to being fed. The baby's survival response relaxes as soon as she's fed.

Unfortunately, many children and adults live with a heightened survival response, constantly worrying about their lives or preparing for the next fight. When this happens, their ability to think clearly, process emotions, and enjoy loving relationships is diminished. Their communication is dominated by reactions, such as aggression (the fight response) or passive aggression (the flight response).

It is possible for those of us with heightened survival responses to free ourselves from that painful cycle. I will show you how when we explore the four layers of communication.

When all three areas of the brain function in harmony, we experience true peace of mind. The easiest way I have found to achieve that peace is to move my attention away from my thoughts toward my body sensations, emotions, and spiritual perception/intuition.

The Body Speaks with Sensations

The images that run through our minds trigger responses in our bodies and emotions. To help them understand this through their own experiences, I once asked participants in a workshop to silently answer these questions: *If there were one conflict or concern distressing you right now, what would it be? Who is involved? What happens when you think about this situation?*

I invited the participants to pay attention to their responses to those questions. I encouraged them to notice how their breathing might have changed, what was happening in their bodies, and whether their thoughts were calm or racing. I paused for a few minutes to allow them time to reflect, and then I asked, "How do you feel now that you've brought this concern to your mind? What is different from five minutes ago?"

Judy, a woman in the audience, called out, "Five minutes ago, I was calm. Now I'm angry!"

I replied, "Good, thank you! Can anyone relate to Judy?" Lots of hands raised, and a few people chuckled as they realized they weren't the only ones who felt worse.

I asked Judy, "When you said that you felt angry, how did you know you felt angry? Was it because in your mind you had that thought? Or was it because in your body you felt something change?"

She replied, "Well, I think I felt it in my body first. My stomach clenched, and my chest got tight."

I then explained to the group that ...

The body responds to information before the rational mind does, but we usually don't notice it.

One reason we don't notice what our bodies are trying to tell us is that it's hard for us to interpret body sensations. Many of us did not grow up learning to notice or understand the language of the body. Instead, we might have been humiliated or reprimanded for responding to body sensations, so we learned to ignore them.

I always felt sorry for my classmate in elementary school who got into trouble for saying he was cold when everyone else felt hot. He also got in trouble for having a hard time sitting still and for sometimes crying for no reason. Now I understand that each of his actions might have been an expression of the language of his body: body sensations that needed to be expressed in order to help him release energy he could not rationalize.

For those who have experienced trauma or who were reprimanded like my classmate, body sensations can feel confusing, overwhelming, even threatening. This certainly was true for me. By the time I reached high school, I had convinced myself that my body was not safe, was not even my own.

When I experienced a body sensation like butterflies in my stomach or tightness in my throat, instead of pausing to notice what I needed or to allow the sensation to pass, I focused on controlling food, exercise, my outward appearance—the only elements of life I felt I could control. I didn't yet have the resources I needed to understand the language of my body and to heal from the emotional and physical trauma I had experienced, so I did the best I could. That's what we all do, isn't it?

When I remember that, it becomes much harder for me to judge myself (or others). We are all doing the best we can, and today's "best" might be different from yesterday's.

Even if you haven't experienced a trauma, you might have become used to dampening your sensitivity to body sensations with things like caffeine, sugar, alcohol, or tobacco. Each of these substances temporarily dulls our awareness. That's why so many of us love them, and it's why it can be so hard to give them up.

The problem occurs when those substances damage our nervous systems, creating a state of constant fight or flight called dysautonomia.[3] Basically, that means that our bodies become stuck in a heightened survival response, and we might suffer from chronically tense muscles, poor sleep, migraines, or irritability.

It took me years to give up diet soda, even though it hurt my stomach and disrupted my sleep. Over and over, I would decide to give it up, but when I felt really stressed or anxious, the craving for diet soda consumed me, and I would give in. Other times, I simply didn't want to feel anxiety, sadness, anger, or even joy, so I would drink a soda, knowing the caffeine would dull my sensitivity for a while. That's the rub, though; the relief was only temporary. Once the caffeine wore off, I was left with an upset stomach, headache, and short temper.

If our bodies want us to pay attention,
they will call upon all their resources, and they won't quit.

We can choose to continue or increase our use of caffeine and other substances, or we can listen to what our bodies are "saying." In the short term, it might be easier to turn to the substance and suffer the consequences later; I've done that many times. In the long term, it is much easier to turn toward the discomfort, because then we can move through the discomfort and gain wisdom.

Until very recently, I ate something for reasons other than hunger every single day. I ate to distract myself from worry or frustration, to experience sweetness in my life, to calm down strong emotions, to escape boredom. In my world, food was rarely just "food."

Sometimes I wished I could be a baby again, discovering my wondrous toes, my busy hands, my "inny" belly button for the first time, without judgment. I wondered what it would be like to sense hunger or thirst and make noise until someone helped me. When I saw a baby completely relaxed in her parent's arms as she napped, I wondered what that might feel like—to totally relax in sleep, rather than hold tension in my muscles, ready to act at any moment, waking at the lightest sound. At other times, I longed to be in my teenage body—slender, nimble, numb.

You see, during my babyhood and childhood, I gradually disconnected from my body until I could no longer hear what it said to me. I no longer recognized shallow breathing and a tight throat as signs of anxiety or tingling in my chest as joy. It did not even occur to me to notice my body sensations. In fact, I wanted nothing to do with my body, because I believed it had betrayed me by attracting dangerous people.

Even hunger and thirst became dull sensations. By age fourteen, I ate and drank according to either the habits of those around me or the protocols of whatever diet I was on at the time. Food had become simply a tool for shaping my body or numbing emotions; eating had nothing to do with hunger or pleasure.

*How do people recover their sensitivity to the way
their body communicates with them?*

I have been discovering my answer to that question for many years. My journey toward a healthy relationship with my body (and food) has included treatment for an eating disorder, in-depth counseling, and spiritual healing.

Now I know that my body belongs to me. I have intellectual knowledge about what and when I "should" eat to be healthy. But I am so much more than my intellect! There is so much communication happening all at once—in my head, heart, body, and spirit—that I can become overwhelmed. When that happens, I either a) escape by eating sugary, fatty foods, or b) pause, notice the body sensations I am experiencing, and ask myself what I need in that moment.

I fully acknowledge that option "a" is my automatic and easiest choice. In fact, when I have been highly stressed, I've eaten half a pizza before consciously noticing that I had even *ordered* a pizza. One of the most helpful realizations I've had about eating unconsciously is that when I do it, I usually have something I want to say or ask, but for some reason, I silence myself instead.

Eating unhealthy food is the primary way
that I silence myself.

When I realized that for the first time, I felt deeply sad. It was like I was viewing a different person. I could see how much this woman wanted to be good, to do well, to please others. I could see that she had truths and feelings to express that were being stifled—stuffed.

Once, I found myself snacking all afternoon at my desk at work. When I asked myself what I was silencing, I noticed that I felt disrespected by my boss, and I was nervous about telling her how I felt. During the next few days, I allowed myself to eat what I craved while I also thought about whether or not to talk to my boss and what I wanted to say to her.

By the third day, I had decided I would talk to my boss, and I had become clear about what I wanted to say. That evening, I found myself cooking vegetables and looking forward to eating them. Rather than trying to control my eating, I had turned my attention toward all the ways in which my body, mind, heart, and intuition were communicating with me.

As I prepared to express my truth, cravings for unhealthy—silencing—foods went away.

Today, when I notice that I am craving or eating unhealthy food, I ask myself, *What am I silencing in myself? Is there something I want to say or ask?* Those questions help me to notice my emotions, my sense of intuition, the thoughts in my mind, and my body sensations.

A whole world of communication opens up. It's as though I can hear myself making noise like the babies who cry for attention.

When I give myself the gift of noticing and responding to my thoughts, emotions, intuition, and body sensations, the urge to eat unhealthy food dissolves.

When we pay attention to our bodies' perception, it becomes much easier to move through discomfort when it occurs. If we rest when we feel tired instead of drinking caffeine, or eat something really nutritious when we're hungry, we will feel nurtured and more balanced. Then, when life throws us a curve ball, we will have the energy and support we need to respond to it.

The Heart Contains Deep Wisdom

What do you normally do when you are at work and you're feeling angry or upset, but you have a job to do? Which one do you give your attention to, the feelings or the job? The job, right? And what do you tell yourself about the feelings?

If you're like most people, you ignore them, you push them away, you think, *It's not that big of a deal; it'll pass.* When we do that to ourselves, especially when we say to ourselves, *Let it go,* or, *This shouldn't bother me …*

*We rob ourselves of the information
that our hearts are trying to give us,
and we store up feelings for our next reaction.*

If I had said to Judy, my workshop participant who told us she felt angry, "You shouldn't be angry," do you think her anger would have increased or decreased? Yes, it would have increased, of course. That's because …

We cannot decrease painful emotions
by focusing on logic or intellect.

You might remember that reactions, such as anger and constant worry, are driven by our survival instinct. They short circuit our rational mind and can cloud our awareness of deeper feelings. Our emotions are connected to our minds and bodies, but they must be addressed through experience in our hearts if we want to learn from and become free of painful reactions.

Sometimes, it might seem like all communication is some form of reaction. That's understandable, since many of us are accustomed to living in reaction. That's exactly what reality shows and soap operas are all about; it's why we love them. People are reacting all over the place, and it's juicy! It's why family gatherings and work places can feel like soap operas too.

The more people ignore their own emotions,
the stronger their reactions become,
and the easier it becomes for them to disregard
other people's emotions.

That's why communication can become very painful. Two people who love each other can get to the point where they exchange hurtful words they would never say to a stranger.

How can that be? Well, over time, people can become disconnected from their deeper feelings. When that happens, they become disconnected from—even threatened by—other people's deeper feelings, too.

If I ignore or minimize my feelings when I am upset, or if I choose not to tell the truth about how I feel, reactions can become "normal." Eventually, I might stop relating to my loved ones in an authentic, intimate manner. When that happens, hurtful words can flow all too easily.

The less I pay attention to my own heart,
the more I blame another person when I feel unhappy,
and it's easy to point the blame close to home.

Communication can shift from painful to nurturing when we include what our hearts are "saying." I'll show you how in each upcoming chapter. As you move through the four layers of communication, you will open up to more of what your heart has to offer you. I've found it to be much more and much better than I ever imagined. My friend Tom discovered this too, one day when we were talking on the phone.

I felt somber and tired that day, so I was more quiet than usual. Tom and I had recently reconnected after years of being out of touch, so we weren't used to each other's patterns yet. After a few minutes, Tom asked me, "What's the matter? Are you upset with me?"

I replied, "No, everything's fine. I'm just feeling quiet today."

That reply did not fit with Tom's mental picture. He was listening to his rational mind, which, you might remember, is designed to identify cause and effect. His mind needed to identify a cause for my somber mood, and since he didn't know me very well, he naturally pointed to himself as the cause.

We tried for several minutes to resolve this tension. I told him again that nothing was wrong, and he asked more questions to try to figure out what I was hiding. Knowing that this mental investigation was not going to resolve anything (since nothing was wrong), I asked Tom if he would be willing to try an experiment. Cautiously, Tom replied, "Okay."

"Thanks," I said. "Right now, your mind is trying to figure out what's going on inside my heart. But the only way you will really know what's going on in my heart is if you listen to my heart, with your own heart.

"Try to relax your mind for a moment," I continued. "Imagine that your heart, the area in the center of your chest, can radiate outward toward me, and that my heart is radiating outward toward you. Imagine that our hearts meet in the middle. Can you imagine that?"

After a brief pause, Tom replied, "Yes, I've got it."

"Good," I continued. "Now, notice how you feel. What's different from a couple of minutes ago?"

Tom said, "It feels like everything's all right, like there's nothing to worry about."

"Exactly!" I responded. "Your heart just listened to mine, and it perceived the truth that everything's all right. Now your mind can catch up to this new information, even though it contradicts the cause-effect pattern you're used to." After that, Tom and I enjoyed a twenty-minute conversation without a hint of the tension that had dominated our attention earlier.

Can you see how much faster Tom opened to the truth that nothing was wrong when he listened to his heart instead of his mind? Even though it was unfamiliar to him, by taking a chance and trying the activity I suggested, Tom saved himself time, energy, and unnecessary discomfort.

Information that would take hours or days to integrate rationally can be clear to us in mere minutes when we listen to our hearts.

The Spirit Speaks Our Personal Truth

You can listen to the communication of your deep inner truth by paying attention to your intuition, whether or not you follow a spiritual path. For those who are skeptical, consider that there are neural cells in our chests and bellies that function very much like those in the brain.[4] In fact, 65 percent of the cells in the heart are neural cells, which make and release their own neurotransmitters and communicate directly with the limbic brain (the emotional mind).[5]

Our intuition is trustworthy.
We can access it in many different ways.

One way is to pay attention to every thought that crosses our minds, especially the ones that we normally would dismiss. The first time I tried that, I was amazed by the results!

When I reached my final year of doctoral studies, it was no longer necessary for me to live near campus, so I decided to move home to Great Falls, Montana, to be near friends and mountains while I wrote my dissertation. I had been reading about the power of intention, so in preparation for my move, I decided to see what would happen if I stated exactly what I wanted and then paid attention to every single thought that crossed my mind.

I wrote down every detail that I wanted to find in my next apartment: old, craftsman-style architecture; original fixtures; warm community; near a park; not on the ground floor; in a corner; with lots of natural sunlight; all for an inexpensive rent. Was I asking too much? Some people thought so, but I figured I had nothing to lose. I decided to believe it was possible that such an apartment existed. Every day, I stated out loud, "My next apartment will be ..." and I stated each of the details I wanted.

When I began calling apartment managers, a certain building came to my mind, one that I had admired several times on visits home. I wondered if they might have an opening and then immediately thought, *No, I'm sure they don't have one. That's a very popular building.* In the past, I would have dropped it and moved on to other apartments. But since I had made a commitment to pay attention to every thought, I decided there must be a reason why that apartment building had come to my mind.

I called the building manager and asked if he had a one-bedroom apartment available. He replied, "No, sorry, I don't." My heart sank a little, until he continued, "But I will have one as of May 31." It just so happened that May 31 was the first day I would need the apartment, so I asked him to describe it to me.

"It's on the second floor, in the northeast corner. It gets lots of sunlight and has all the original fixtures from the 1930s. We've got a real nice community here, just a block from the best park in town. Some tenants have lived here for decades." And how much was the rent? Three hundred and fifty dollars.

I can't believe this! I said to myself, and then I quickly followed up with *Yes, I can believe it. It's perfectly natural, because my intuition is trustworthy.* I asked a friend to walk through the apartment for me to make sure it was nice, and then I rented it over the phone.

The next day, I was working on my computer when the question crossed my mind: *I wonder if I have to give notice on the apartment I'm in before moving out.* Immediately, I thought, *No, surely not. It's a university apartment. They must know that people leave at the end of the academic year.*

In the past, I would have believed my own assumptions and not checked. Instead, I again decided to trust that there was a reason for every thought that crossed my mind. I called the apartment office to ask if I had to give notice. "Yes," was the reply. "You have to give sixty days' notice, in writing."

"I'll be right over!" I cried. I quickly hung up the phone and ran to the office. It was five minutes before closing, exactly sixty days from the date I planned to move out.

Spiritual Perception

Someone once told me that people from every culture who seek spiritual truth will find it right where they are, and I agree. For some, the path is narrow and straight. For others, like me, it's curved and broad. My path has helped me learn the language of my spirit. If you would like to listen in on my communication with the divine, read on, knowing that my path might be different from yours and might bump up against your spiritual ideals. Or, simply skip this section and go on to enjoy the following chapters.

I have been a spiritual seeker since I was very young. As a child in elementary school, I often walked to my neighborhood Episcopal church by myself for Sunday services. I liked church because the people were nice, I enjoyed singing hymns, and I wanted to know God. I had a deep sense that God existed, that some "one" greater than me was always near, was loving, and was watching (that part made me nervous).

I remember adults smiling at me with a look of curiosity in their eyes, as if they wondered, *What is this nine-year-old girl doing in church, sitting so quietly by herself?* The answer was simple: I felt comforted in church. I wondered who exactly God was and how I could know him. And, I wondered how I could be good enough to be loved completely; I wanted to learn the rules.

I'm aware that these might not be typical questions for a nine-year-old, but they were persistent for me, and at that age, I felt no self-consciousness about my search. Over time, I attended Christian churches of various denominations. Joining friends and their families, I experienced Catholic, nondenominational, Baptist, and evangelical faith communities. In each one, I found answers to some of my questions, but no matter how fervently I accepted what a church taught me, a nagging discomfort remained. Rather than increasing, my sense of worthiness declined as I learned more of the rules and recognized my persistent imperfections.

By the time I entered college, I had firmly rooted myself in Christianity. Before my freshman classes began, I found a college group to join that I believed would protect me from my "sinful impulses" (like dating wild boys and partying). That group provided a fun, safe, friendly community for me, and it provided excellent training in leadership skills.

Unfortunately, it also provided strong reinforcement of my belief that I had to be perfect in order to be worthy of the love and forgiveness I craved. Their rhetoric matched my internal voice: "God's love is unconditional, but 'faith without works is dead,' so you'd better keep demonstrating more and better actions." In other words: you are not enough.

The local church I joined emphasized what we members should be doing—always more and better than before. Of course I was drawn to that church, because their message mirrored my belief that I was not enough. When my heart was in pain, if I turned to a church or college group leader for support, they talked to me about thoughts and actions, not feelings, body sensations, or spiritual perception.

Over time, I believed I was a little more worthy than before because I followed all the rules. At the same time, I felt more separate than ever because of my past, my fears, and what I saw as my faults. This was a wretched way to live, yet until I reached my thirties, I did not open to another possibility.

Another snag for me was that, deep down, I did not believe there could be just one way to know God. I doubted whether a God who had infused his creation with brilliant, beautiful, limitless diversity would provide just one approach to knowing him.

Every culture around the world cultivates spiritual beliefs; that truth affirmed my sense that God did indeed exist, and it challenged the idea that Christianity was the only way to know God. I believed in Jesus, and still do, just not in the way my church described him.

Eventually, I realized that, for me, the Christian path was too focused on mental processing and doing, and I could not agree with its exclusivity. I needed support and guidance to connect with my heart and learn the language of my soul.

During the first ten years after college, I lived in several different states, from New York to Texas. With each move, I started a new job and continued my spiritual quest by reading books and occasionally visiting faith communities. I felt very lonely, yet also very cautious. I longed to know God in my whole being, not just my mind. I wanted to know God through my own experience, rather than someone else's advice or interpretation.

Later in the book, you will read other stories from my life and learn how a perfect storm of crises propelled me into a life-changing relationship with a wonderful counselor. I was thirty-three and living in Austin when I began working with Rebecca. Not only was Rebecca a licensed counselor, she also was a master Sufi teacher and a student of Somatic Experiencing®, which is a very gentle yet effective approach to healing trauma in the body.

With Rebecca's help, I began to learn the language of my body, my heart, and (thank God, finally!) my soul. I had worked with many counselors before, never achieving anything like the relief and peace I was beginning to know in my work with Rebecca. My progress with her was so gentle, yet so efficient, that one day I asked her what made the difference. Rebecca explained the Sufi principles that undergirded her approach to therapy, and I became more and more intrigued.

Austin was a wonderful melting pot for healers of all kinds, so I had lots of options to explore. I attended workshops given by spiritual leaders and learned more about Sufi spiritual healing as well as Jewish faith communities and Buddhist practices.

After a year or so, I decided to attend the University of Spiritual Healing and Sufism. Before my first week of school, I set an intention to heal one of the major traumas I had suffered as a teenager. I prayed and asked God to support me, to protect me, and to help me open to whatever he wanted me to experience. I felt nervous but hopeful.

Each day of the week-long school session, I learned new healing practices, including Remembrance, which I will teach you in the chapter about the fourth layer of communication. Even though I felt nervous and uncertain about this path called Sufism, I felt I had nothing to lose—I had lived in emotional and spiritual agony for so long. I felt comforted by the fact that I did not have to become a Sufi in order to benefit from the healing practices, and I was willing to trust, little by little, because of the profound healing I already had experienced in my work with Rebecca.

On the third day, I was paired with a woman named Kim to learn a new practice. I can't remember exactly what the practice involved, but I remember it was very simple. When she was the "healer" and I was the "healee," she simply sat with me and prayed silently as I asked God to help me know, really know, that I was forgiven (at that time, I felt responsible for the trauma I had suffered). Neither of us spoke. Kim did not know what caused my suffering or of what I yearned to be healed. She didn't need to know, because God was the real healer; she was a support, a conduit.

As we prayed, each in our own way, I asked God to show me the truth. Over and over again, I silently asked, *Please show me the truth. Please show me the truth.* While I prayed, images came to my mind. I saw myself as a sixteen-year-old after the trauma. At first, the scene was dim, and I saw myself in grey silhouette, and then it was flooded with golden light. I clearly saw Jesus embracing me and felt myself melt into his arms, sobbing from fear, despair, and relief.

With my new friend sitting beside me, silently supporting me, I began weeping and could not stop myself, did not want to stop myself. Even when the faculty called the group back together to debrief the healing session, I continued to weep, my head resting in my folded arms, waves of grief being followed by waves of peace. No one asked me to stop. No one asked me to explain myself. No one tried to quiet my tears. It was exactly what I needed.

That experience left a permanent impression on my spirit, heart, body, and mind. After that, I felt no doubt about whether or not God existed, no doubt about whether or not God loved me, no doubt about whether or not Jesus was real. The "knowledge" had arrived through my spirit first, and then as I wept, my heart, body, and mind had integrated it.

That's why it worked so well for me; my sharp mind had relaxed enough for me to bring in new information—information that changed the old cause-effect beliefs (*e.g., That happened to me because I did something wrong*). I had tried many times to change those beliefs by changing my thinking but had never succeeded.

This time, my thinking changed in response to the communication in my spirit and my heart. Sufism is a spiritual path that accesses divine light through the heart first, allowing the mind to catch up. That worked for me, and I have continued on a Sufi path ever since. That does not mean that I now subscribe to Sufism as the only way to know God; that claim would be contrary to my intuition and Sufism itself. Rather, I have found a path that helps me to communicate with and from my spirit. Everyone who seeks spiritual truth will find it, right where they are, because it already exists within them.

I shared this story with you not to convince you to explore a particular spiritual path, but simply to illustrate what I experience when I listen to my spirit: my body relaxes, my thoughts change from being negative or painful to being comforting and peaceful, and my emotions flow freely.

When we connect deeply with our spirit/intuition, all of the organs of perception come into harmony. We are aware of thoughts, but they do not dominate. We notice what our bodies are telling us, and we do not try to change it. We feel every emotion as it comes, without trying to hold on to the ones that feel good or ignore the ones that feel bad. We listen to our intuition, because we realize that it is trustworthy. And, if we have a spiritual practice, we feel a deeper connection to divine support. Each of the four organs of perception holds immense power.

*The mind, body, heart, and spirit/intuition perceive
different nuances of information.
When we learn their language and choose to listen,
they help us to experience life more fully.*

Sometimes we might get stuck in our thoughts, unwilling to open our hearts—that's what happens in layer one of communication. Other times, we might experience peace as we open up to the full spectrum of communication that occurs within us and between us and others—that's what happens in layer four. In each of the four layers of communication, we pay attention to our mind, body, heart, and spirit/intuition differently.

The Four Layers of Communication

My system for understanding and improving communication is organized into four layers because when we communicate, we tend to pay attention to one of our four organs of perception more than the others. Depending on the topic and the other people involved, we give more credit to the information coming from our mind (layer one), body (layer two), heart (layer three), or spirit/ intuition (layer four). In essence ...

The four layers of communication are
different degrees of connection with our own truth.

No layer is better or worse than any other. Rather, when we communicate from a layer, the results are either what we want or what we don't want (which isn't the same thing as good or bad.

Everything is good if it helps us get in touch with who we really are.)

It's helpful for me to notice which layer I am in at any moment, because then I can better understand what lies beneath the surface within myself and decide how to address it. As we explore the four layers of communication together, I will share with you some of my personal stories and a few from my clients to illustrate what's really going on in communication.

I will describe each layer separately because that helps me to understand my attitudes and needs, but I hope you will see from the stories that it is normal to move from layer one (mind) to four (spirit/intuition) and back to one (mind) again in just a few moments.

What I want, for myself and for you, is awareness. Awareness of what the four layers of communication are, what they feel like, and what we experience when we choose to communicate from each one of them. With that awareness ...

We have the power to experience
what we really want, moment by moment,
and to communicate in the healthiest, most effective manner.

To begin each of the following chapters, I provide a summary of what I personally experience in that layer. If my summaries help you, consider writing your own summaries as you become familiar with what happens inside of you in each layer of communication.

Layer One: *I want what I want, and I am right.*

My core belief is:
I am not enough.

My mind tells me:
I am not _____ enough.
There is not enough _____ for me.
You are a threat to me.

I feel:
Anxious
Unsafe
Alone

I project onto you:
Criticism
Judgment

When I consider a conflict from layer one,
I see:
Roadblocks
And I:
Blame you
Debate you

Most of the time, most people are thinking and communicating from this layer, so it's important to know what layer one feels like to you and how to recognize it in another person. Layer one is driven by the survival instinct, which means that reaction determines almost everything. When we are in reaction, adrenaline floods our bodies, and it feels like we know everything—that we are right—but we are missing a lot of the information that is available in our emotions, body sensations, and intuition.

If our survival were threatened, this exclusive focus on reaction might save our lives because we wouldn't waste energy on rational thoughts or emotions. In daily life, however ...

Being unaware of our deeper feelings, body sensations,
thoughts, and intuition can lead to an overall
sense of fatigue, unhappiness, or unease.

When I am in layer one and people are watching me communicate, they might think that my only interest is in what I want. This is easy to see when children fight over a toy. If we look for it, it is easy to see between adults, too.

I want what I want! and *I am right!* are not bad thoughts. They are part of our survival instinct, which is a brilliant gift from the divine universe that keeps us alive. The core belief that drives layer one of communication is this: *I am not enough.* We may not be aware of this belief, but we can find it if we tune into our thoughts, because our core beliefs drive our thoughts.

In layer one, our thoughts might tell us, *I am not rich enough, intelligent enough, brave enough, beautiful enough, thin enough ...*

I don't have enough … I don't have enough beef … I need a new car … I don't have enough money. Have you ever thought any of those things? Me, too.

A lot of people are in competition for attention, money, and goods, because our culture generates the belief that there isn't enough. Companies often create the illusion of scarcity to drive sales, and boy does it work, like at Christmas time when there is a toy that every parent is trying to get for his or her child.

In 1983, the hot item was the Cabbage Patch doll. In 2007, it was the video game system called the Wii. I knew parents who were calling all over town to find the Wii, anxious with worry that their children would be disappointed on Christmas Day. Even if they had been in a board meeting, they would have left to go get the Wii, because there weren't enough to go around.

When that perception of "not enough" spreads, stories appear on the news chronicling the battles that parents get into over these toys. You can almost hear their minds screaming, *I want what I want, and I want it right now!* Everyone seems prepared for a fight in layer one.

Remember, layer one is driven by the survival instinct,
which heightens our reactions.

Anyone who has a contrary opinion to ours feels like a threat. In me, this creates a sense of anxiety; my stomach gets in knots, and I feel separated from others. When I really pay attention, I recognize that I feel alone.

In her powerful book, *Hands of Light*, Barbara Brennan says, "All pain is caused by the illusion of separateness, which leads to fear and self-hatred."[6] For me, it's true. Every time I am in a lot of pain, I realize I am thinking something negative about myself or I am fearful. Usually, I'm fearful there won't be enough for me.

As I approached forty and wasn't yet a mother, I had to deal with thoughts like, *There's not enough time for me,* and, *There aren't enough partners for me to have a partner.* Thoughts like these reinforced my experience of anxiety and my evaluation of myself as not being enough to have what I deeply wanted. I became caught in what I call the Reaction Cycle: I observe something or interact with someone. Then I experience a reaction. Then I wait for it to happen again, and the cycle starts over again.

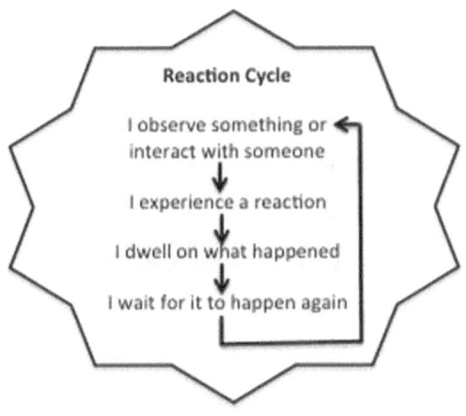

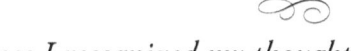

Once I recognized my thoughts as forms of reaction,
I made room for what I would rather believe.

Since I did not have the ability to predict the future, I decided I would rather believe that there was plenty of time for me and that I would find a partner who was right for me. Every time I noticed myself worrying about running out of time, I repeated my new mantra out loud: "There is plenty of time for me." That practice really helped. Eventually, the worrisome thoughts stopped showing up in my head. I freed myself from that reaction cycle.

Sometimes we can move out of reaction by changing our thoughts. Other times, particularly when we are in reaction toward someone else, forgiveness can help us move beyond reaction so we can see what's below the surface inside ourselves.

Forgiveness can be very helpful, because it releases us. In fact, the Greek word for forgiveness means "release from bondage or imprisonment."[7] It is not about emotion; it is about choice. I learned this soon after moving into my first apartment in Missoula, Montana.

I had selected the apartment very carefully. Before sending in a deposit, I had spent time in reflection, asking for guidance and clarifying my intuition about it. After having felt certain that this was the place for me, I was very surprised by what I found when I arrived at my new home.

First, the apartment lacked most of the amenities listed on the property's website. When I pointed this out to the manager, he abruptly showed me the fine print that read, "Not all amenities available in some units." The manager and I got off to a great start!

From our first conversation, both of us were in reaction, each of us wanting what we wanted and believing we were right.

The next thing that upset me was that my apartment lacked windows in the living room. I had heard that Missoula could be gloomy in the winter, so I had made a point of confirming in advance that I would get a unit with vaulted ceilings and large windows in the living room. Neither was part of my new home.

The angrier and more demanding I got, the more determined the property manager was not to help me. I asked to be let out of my lease; he refused. Within days, I had contacted a lawyer and was prepared to spend my savings in order to get out of that apartment. When I drove home after work each day, I dreaded entering the property, and I fantasized about confronting (read: flattening) the manager.

One day, it occurred to me that while I had been surprised by the conditions of my new apartment and the attitude of the manager, God hadn't. I had asked for guidance while looking for a place, and I had sensed without a doubt that I was supposed to live there. So I concluded that this experience must have come for my good.

Something was being mirrored to me.

I paused for reflection. When I asked myself how I should move forward, the first thing that came to my mind was the word "forgiveness" and the image of the property manager. I trusted that this response was the voice of my deeper knowing, my spiritual intuition.

I took a deep breath and said out loud, "I choose to forgive this man, even though he may not think he has wronged me and even though he is not sorry for the way he has treated me. I release him. He no longer owes me anything. I choose to believe that everything will be okay, even though this apartment does not match my expectations."

The next day, I canceled proceedings with my lawyer. I started to relax in my decision to make the best of it. Within days, I noticed that my reactions to what the manager said or did were softer, and I was no longer distracted by the situation.

Two weeks later, he was replaced by a new manager who turned out to be a wonderful resource for me and the other residents. I love this part of moving through reaction …

When we turn toward what is bothering us and recognize our part, the source of the reflection softens or goes away.

I got out of the reaction cycle of layer one by taking the focus off of my apartment and the property manager and turning it toward my part. When I became willing to forgive, everything changed. I stayed in the apartment through the end of my lease and even made some good friends in the complex.

As my apartment story illustrates, when I am in layer one, I blame others for my problems, and I am much more likely to get into a debate, because I believe that I am right. If another person tosses out an idea, I am going to be quick to jump on it and say why it won't work. I am also likely to criticize and judge. Why would I do that? Because it is a reflection of what I am doing to myself.

One of my clients, Jack, was dogged by the belief, *I am not capable of being a good manager.* For months, he refused to challenge that statement because he believed it so strongly, and because it was too painful. Then one day, Jack complained to me that another one of his employees was undermining him and making him look incapable.

I reminded Jack that life is a mirror of the core beliefs we hold about ourselves, and I asked him, "Didn't you tell me that you feel incapable of being a good manager?"

"Yes," he replied.

I then told him, "As long as you hold onto that belief, your brain will look for evidence to support it. It wouldn't matter if you had a dream team on your staff, you would still find evidence that your management skills were being called into question, because you are questioning them every day."

I explained that it's like when someone has his eye on a particular car he wants to own. As soon as he decides that's the car he wants, he starts seeing cars just like it all over town. That's because …

When we make a decision, our brains seek out information to support that decision and bring it to its fullest expression.[8]

As the very popular book and movie *The Secret* points out, you can use this to your advantage. Elite athletes do it all the time when they visualize the perfect performance. Over and over again, research has shown that such visualization positively impacts performance.[9] But *The Secret* is missing a crucial piece of the puzzle.

*Getting what you want brings only fleeting satisfaction
if you carry painful beliefs about
your worthiness or enoughness.*

That's why the phrase "Money doesn't buy happiness" rings true. Too much is never enough, because nothing outside ourselves can make up for the painful beliefs we hold about our worthiness and enoughness.

Someone with the core belief *I am not enough* will always worry that the wealth will not last. They will worry that someday there will not be enough for them, so they will focus on getting more, when what they really want is to relax, know they are safe, and enjoy what they have acquired. That is possible, but not in layer one.

As you get to know yourself better, you will begin to recognize reaction when it hits you. Until then, it might help to watch for these common signs of reaction:

- Irritability
- Intense anger that outweighs the situation
- Despair
- "Always" and "Never" thinking
- Worry
- Perfectionism
- Self-criticism

I know these well, because I used to experience them every day. Growing up, reactions were so common in my home that I did not stop to question whether or not they were reasonable. The only difference between my emotional reactions and those of my parents was that mine were not expressed. No one else knew the intensity of my reactions, because I did not show or express my feelings. Instead, I rationalized everything by creating reasons for everyone's behavior.

One of the things that strongly triggered me was when one of my parents, usually my father, was late. He even missed my senior cello recital, and I was the last performer! I remember the moment he staggered into the recital hall: I met him in the back of the room as I walked out.

When he looked at me with bloodshot eyes, he smiled as if he felt proud to have made it at all. I did not smile when I stated matter-of-factly, "You missed it." I did not tell him I felt hurt, disappointed, and angry. Instead, I held in my feelings, as usual, and we went home.

By the time I got to college, I was extremely sensitive to timeliness but did not know why. Regardless of the reason, if I was late by just one minute, I felt deeply guilty, and if a friend was a few minutes late meeting me, I felt angry. One Saturday morning as I waited outside for two friends to pick me up for a trip to the mall, I noticed myself becoming intensely angry when I realized they were two minutes late.

As my watch ticked off the seconds, my thoughts raced. I thought of all the hurtful reasons why they could be late. *They're playing a joke on me. They forgot me. They don't really care about me.* These thoughts swirled in my mind as I became more anxious and indignant. Then, something happened that I had not experienced before. A new thought entered my mind: *What if it isn't about me? Maybe they're just late.*

That possibility interrupted my racing thoughts so I could pause and take a deep breath. Then I thought to myself, *I wonder why I get so angry when people are late.* Immediately, scenes of my parents being late or expressing irritation at having to drive me somewhere filled my mind. That's when I realized that …

I had been projecting onto my friends
the disappointment and anger
I felt toward my parents.

Because I had never told my mom or dad the truth about how I felt, my feelings had become impacted like a wisdom tooth. Anything that even slightly resembled an experience I had had with my parents triggered those old emotions and insecurities. That day, thanks to my friends' lateness, I had the chance to absorb this new awareness and release myself from my reaction.

As my friends arrived to pick me up, they yelled out the car window, "Annie!" and cheered. If I had not paused to wonder about my reaction, I would not have trusted their joy in seeing me. But since I had moved through my reaction, I was able to feel and trust the love they had for me, relax, and have fun.

When you recognize them, you will be able to move through reactions too. Experiment with the tips included at the end of this chapter, if you'd like. Eventually, I'm sure you will identify strategies that work for you. Being curious really helps.

The quickest way I have found to move through reaction is to pause, take a deep breath, and ask myself what I need. Sometimes, I don't know what I need in the moment, but by asking myself the question, my attention shifts from other people or events (which I cannot control) toward myself.

I become able to notice my emotions, body sensations, and intuition, and that shift reconnects me with my inner truth and my power.

If you find yourself focusing on or complaining about someone, you can shift out of reaction by asking yourself questions, such as: *What is my irritation really about? What do I need in this moment? What do I really want right now?*

If you ask yourself those questions, you might realize that you really want to say or ask something of that person. You might want to know that you are loved, that you matter. If that's the case, you might call your favorite person to connect. If you are far from friends or family or don't feel like talking to people, animals can be great nurturers.

Have you ever noticed that pets know when their human friends are sad? Dogs, especially, take great delight in expressing love, so if there are no people you want to reach out to, consider going to an animal shelter or pet store to snuggle with a puppy if you don't have a pet at home. An added benefit of connecting with animals is that they don't require any explanation. They don't care why we're snuggling or playing with them, they are just glad to be with us.

*The more you practice pausing, the easier it will be
to choose what you really want for yourself.*

When you do that, communicating with others will be much easier, too. Remember to be gentle with yourself and go slowly.

It takes time to change habits, and it can feel risky to acknowledge what lies beneath the surface or pursue what we really want. I have been working on this for years. Every day, it seems I learn something new about myself or someone I love.

Layer one of communication is important and valuable. Our survival instinct keeps us safe. It helps us respond to threat by flooding our muscles with adrenaline and interrupting our ability to think rationally and process emotions. In a situation like being cut off in traffic, this instinct is really helpful. Instantly, we forget about everything except controlling our vehicle and steering toward safety.

*The key is to pause after the threat has passed,
acknowledge our feelings,
allow the adrenaline to stop flowing,
and then pay attention to what we need.*

When we do that, we move into the deeper layers of communication, which are equally as valuable—and a lot more fun.

What to Do When Someone Else Is in Layer One

When people we work with or live with are stuck in layer one, it can be tempting to join them in reaction. Anger and resentment build, and it feels good to blow off steam—for a moment. Then, working or living together becomes uncomfortable, and we might start to avoid each other.

The first thing you can do if someone else is in layer one is to make sure that you move through your own reaction. Otherwise, your communication with that person will simply be an exchange of reactions, and your frustration will get worse. Next, ask yourself if you want to set a boundary with that person. Healthy boundaries are very supportive of healthy communication.

If someone regularly tells you what to do, criticizes you, or hurts you, it is probably time for a healthy boundary.

How do you set a boundary? By speaking your truth in a clear, loving way. To help, I have provided tips at the end of this chapter.

Keep in mind that if you speak from reaction, you will get more reaction in return. But if you speak from your heart, you might be surprised by the response. Let me be clear that speaking from your heart does not mean being weak. It simply means being kind.

Do you remember the story of my 1930s cottage? My neighbor took up space easily, and I saw my reflection. You know how that led to a breakthrough for me, but you don't yet know the rest of the story.

Four days after my neighbor gave notice that she would move out, I came home to find the blossoms missing from the flowers on my front steps. I also noticed that some important mail was on the ground.

When I got settled inside, I heard my neighbor arrive. She slammed her door four times and yelled out, "I'm back!" (She had been out of town.)

Immediately, I went into reaction and shouted, "Why do you do that? It's so rude!"

My adrenaline was pumping. I jumped out of my chair and stomped on the floor (her ceiling). Then I played the worst music I could find as loudly as my stereo would go, and I turned up our common thermostat to ninety degrees. I knew none of that would motivate my neighbor to be more considerate, but in that moment, I didn't care! I was enjoying my reaction!

Once I had gotten it out of my system (and become really sick of that awful music), I paused to look beneath the surface. *I wonder what my reaction is really about,* I thought.

The first thing that came to my mind was that I was concerned my neighbor might damage my property or threaten my safety. Her behavior had been so illogical, I didn't know what to expect. I decided I needed to set a boundary.

I pulled out a piece of paper and wrote to her in clear, nonthreatening language. I told her I had noticed the blossoms missing from my flowers and the mail on the ground. I then told her that if any other property of mine became missing or damaged, I would call the police immediately.

I did not accuse her of causing the damage. I simply stated the truth that I would call the police if there were any further damage. Then I said that I chose to live in peace in my home; if she chose to continue slamming doors and blasting her music, I would not retaliate.

I taped the letter to her door and then promptly left town for four days! (I'm courageous but not superhuman.) During my long weekend, my mind wandered through various anxiety-induced fantasies. In one, the house went up in flames. In another, I tripped on booby traps inside my living room. Eventually, I accepted the fact that I had no control over what my neighbor would do.

What do you think happened when I got home? I was a little worried, not knowing if her reactions would become even more extreme, but I felt better knowing that I had set a clear boundary without making her wrong or bad.

I had simply stated my truth in a clear, loving way. She may not have felt it was loving, but by withholding judgment and accusations, I was expressing love. And, by setting the boundary and making the decision to live in peace, I was expressing love for myself. I no longer would be a candidate for that particular reaction cycle.

Believe it or not, she didn't slam her door or blast her stereo again, until the day she moved out. She left with a final slam of the door, and I rented the whole house.

It used to be very hard for me to set boundaries; I felt nervous and guilty when I tried. Now it's easy, if I take time to prepare and then speak my truth in a clear, respectful way.

The next time you recognize that you are in reaction,
see if you can pause long enough
to ask yourself if you need to set a new boundary.

It can feel uncomfortable at first, especially if painful beliefs are driving your thoughts. But, if you take plenty of time to prepare and experiment with the tips on the next few pages, you might find it easier than you expect.

Tips for Moving through Layer One

PRACTICE SELF-RESPONSIBILITY.
Only you are responsible for your reactions and choices. You are only responsible for *your* reactions and choices.

PAUSE, TAKE A BREATH, AND LET IT OUT GENTLY.
This will allow some of the pent-up energy to release.

SEE IF YOU CAN NOTICE WHAT YOUR BODY FEELS LIKE.
Are you cold, hot, relaxed, tight, trembling, sleepy? Is your breathing deep or shallow, slow or quick? There is no need to change anything; simply noticing body sensations helps us become grounded.

Over forty years of research by Dr. Peter Levine has shown that these are natural actions of the nervous system when the body releases energy that was generated by the survival response.[10] For more information about the body's natural instinct to heal, see Dr. Levine's excellent book, *Waking the Tiger: Healing Trauma: The Innate Capacity to Transform Overwhelming Experiences.*

NOTICE YOUR FEET: HOW THEY FEEL, WHERE THEY ARE.
Wiggle your toes. This one is fun and really effective. When we are in reaction, our ability to think rationally is interrupted by the survival responses of fight, flight, and freeze. Thoughts can race as the mind reviews our history and predicts what will happen next.

Anyone can begin to feel overwhelmed, and it's natural to try to reason with ourselves, to think our way to a solution. The thing is, we can't think our way out of reaction. Instead, try giving your attention to your feet!

Ask yourself, *Where are my feet right now?* Be as specific as you can with your answer to help your mind be where your feet are. This is really helpful when you are trying to fall asleep but can't because your thoughts are racing. If you wiggle your toes and observe where your body is in that moment, soon your mind will figure out that you are not in the past and you are not in the future, you are in bed. Then you can choose to "be" in bed.

LOOK AROUND YOU.
Notice what is around you, what the sky (or ceiling) looks like. Take in as many details as possible to help your mind return to the present moment.

STATE OUT LOUD TODAY'S DATE, THE TIME, WHERE YOU ARE, AND WHAT YOU ARE DOING IN THIS MOMENT.
This is another tip to help bring you back to the present moment and allow your fight, flight, or freeze response to relax. Again, the more specific you are, the more quickly your mind will open and your reaction will diminish.

BE CAREFUL NOT TO FOCUS ON BLAME.
If you believe that you or someone else is at fault, you will give your power away, and your reaction will get stronger. Instead, hold your perception up to a higher source of light and wisdom. This will interrupt the mind talking to the mind, so you can notice the communication occurring in your heart and spirit. You might ask, "Is it in my highest good to continue believing _____?" and

then notice the first thing that occurs to you. (See the following chapters for more examples of how to clarify your perception.)

PAY ATTENTION TO THE STORIES YOU TELL (ESPECIALLY THE ONES YOU TELL YOURSELF!).

Whatever you dwell on will expand. If you don't like how the stories you tell impact you, ask yourself what you would rather dwell on.

ASK SOMEONE FOR SUPPORT OR PLAY WITH AN ANIMAL.

Remember Barbara Brennan's observation that all pain and suffering are caused by the illusion of separateness. You can break through that illusion by reaching out for support.

SEE IF YOU CAN NOTICE YOUR EMOTIONS.

Do you feel happy, sad, anxious, yearning? Do your best to make room for your emotions without judgment. Are you too distracted by your thoughts or fears to pay attention to your emotions? Whatever you notice, you might say to yourself, *This is good*, as a way of validating that you are okay, just as you are.

Emotions, body sensations, and thoughts are simply forms of information.
There is no benefit to judging some as bad,
because all of them can help us to know ourselves and connect with others.

Tips for Setting Clear Boundaries

Take plenty of time to prepare.

- Make sure you are not in reaction when you set the boundary.
- Remember to pause if you feel yourself going into reaction.

Write down what you want to say first.

- Describe the behavior that you will accept and the behavior you will not accept.
- State what you are willing to do.
- Be clear about how you will respond if this boundary is not respected.
- You can vent reactions on paper first, if you need to, and then tear that up and write down what you might say to set the boundary in a clear, respectful way.

Avoid starting sentences with "You."

- Most people become defensive when boundaries are set with sentences that begin with "You." Plus, when we begin sentences with "You," we reinforce the sense that the other person has all of the power.
- Notice the differences among the following sentences. Say them out loud and notice how powerless or powerful you feel with each one. Then, say them again and notice how you might feel if someone else said each sentence to you.
    1. "You should not yell at me."
    2. "I will leave the room if you yell at me."
    3. "I will leave the room if you yell at me, and I will stay if you speak gently."

Talk to a trusted friend or counselor.

- Especially if boundaries are new to you, it can really help to have someone else's perspective and encouragement.

Remind yourself that you are worthy of respect and love.

- It's true.

Layer Two: *I want what you want, and I am right.*

God, grant me the serenity
to accept the things I cannot change,
the courage to change the things I can,
and the wisdom to know the difference.[11]
~Serenity Prayer

My core belief is:
I am not quite enough.

My mind tells me:
I will be enough when _____.
I am not worthy of _____.
You are worth more than I am.

I feel:
Confused
Overwhelmed
Unseen
Alone

I project onto you:
It's my fault.
It's my responsibility.

When I consider a conflict from layer two,
I see:
More work for myself
And I:
Talk about you

When I am in layer two, someone listening to me might think that I want what they want. That's good, right? Well, let's see …

Are you in a position of serving others? If you are in a position of leadership or in a service industry, or if you are part of a family or in a friendship, you are in a position of serving others, at least some of the time.

*Those of us who are in service tend to believe
that it is our job to take care of others.*

Very often, we also think, *I'll take care of myself later*, but later doesn't come. That's because in layer two, our core belief is, *I am not quite enough.* Sometimes it seems like we are enough just as we are, but we fear that if people really knew us, they would see that we are not quite enough. When we're in layer two, our minds tell us, *I'll be enough when_____.*

Mary was a forty-three-year-old manager and single mother who came to me for help one afternoon. When she arrived, I was struck by her beauty and by her worried blue eyes.

She slumped into a chair with her eyes cast down, heaved a deep sigh, and then timidly said, "I don't know what else to do. I'm exhausted and confused." When I asked her what was wrong, Mary explained that she was a public school administrator, responsible for three subject areas.

"The teachers in two of my departments love me," she said. "They think I'm a fabulous leader. The problem is, the teachers in my third department think I'm a terrible leader, and they constantly complain about me. I don't understand it." Mary's story is a great example of how life reflects our core beliefs about ourselves.

Life offers experiences that confirm our core beliefs about ourselves and experiences that contradict those beliefs.

The teachers in Mary's third department confirmed her belief that she was not enough. At the same time, the teachers in her other departments contradicted that belief by showing appreciation for what she did, without demanding more.

After describing her employees, Mary shifted from the topic of work to family. She spoke with pride about her teenage daughter, yet she seemed even more disheartened and fatigued. Mary said, "I love my daughter, and I know that she loves me, but I always just feel like I'm failing her. I can't stop worrying that I'll do something to mess up her life."

Do you sense a pattern in Mary's comments about her employees and her daughter? I did, and I suggested Mary write down these statements: "They think I'm doing enough, but they're wrong. It feels like enough to them, but it really isn't."

She wrote down the statements, and then I asked her, "Would you say that, in general, those statements are true for you?"

"Yes," she replied.

I asked, "What about when you think of your daughter?"

"Yes."

"And how about with the teachers who are happy with your leadership?"

"Yes."

We had identified one of Mary's core statements:
"I am not doing enough, even if other people think I am."

Can you see how this statement comes from a belief that she is not quite enough? Through her daughter and satisfied teachers, life was reflecting the truth that Mary was enough, but she was telling herself, "Nope, that's not true." That response reinforced her pain and confusion.

We all hold core statements about ourselves. They run in our minds like music in an elevator—at first they are distracting, but eventually we can become unaware that they even exist.

Being unaware of statements that are critical
or demeaning can be dangerous,
because they close us off from love.

I told Mary, "If you want the unhappy teachers to stop complaining, you could focus on what is outside of yourself by establishing more rules, and getting people in higher layers of leadership to enforce those rules. Or, you could be kind to yourself and heal the core statement that you are not doing enough.

"If you do that," I continued, "the people in your unhappy department will shift naturally. It's completely amazing, and I've seen it happen over and over again. Some of them might leave, and others will respond differently to you because your demeanor will have changed. Remember, your employees are your mirror, just as you are theirs."

When you open yourself to love by healing
the statement that you are not doing enough,
you will no longer need a mirror
to reflect the pain that statement creates.

Mary looked at me with an expression that suggested she felt hopeful and scared at the same time. I sensed that she really wanted to believe me.

For years, Mary's mind had repeated and reinforced the core statement, *I will be enough when I do more for them*—for her daughter, for her friends, for her employees. Her mind also had developed the core statement: *I am not worthy of praise.* Even though Mary's daughter and some of her teachers praised her, she did not receive it, because she believed she was not worthy. That reinforced her feeling of being unappreciated. What a painful cycle!

Mary was projecting onto others the layer-two statement: *You are worth more than I am.* This led to her feeling confused and overwhelmed, because she was already doing as much as she could, but to Mary, it wasn't enough. I used to do this to myself all the time and then wonder why I was so exhausted.

"How can I change the belief that I'm not doing enough?" Mary asked me. In reply, I guided her through the following exercise. If you'd like, try it yourself. It might be easier if you ask a friend to read the instructions to you.

Elevator Exercise

To begin, put both feet on the floor and relax into your chair to help you become grounded in your body. Then, close your eyes, because it's easier to relax the mind and connect to the heart when our eyes are closed.

Imagine that there is an elevator at the top of your head. As you imagine the elevator slowly descending to the center of your chest, your attention will naturally flow to your heart, and you may begin to feel relaxed.

Imagine yourself stepping out of the elevator into warm, nurturing sunlight. As the light gently envelops you, ask, either silently or aloud, *Is it true that I am not doing enough?* (Or, insert your own statement after *Is it true that* _____.)

Pay attention to the first thing that comes to your mind after asking that question. The reason it's important to notice the first thing that comes to your mind is ...

The wisdom of our hearts often contradicts the statements in our minds.

If we don't pay attention to the first answer, which in Mary's case was, *You are doing enough*, our minds quickly jump in with all the reasons why the first answer can't be true. The next time you recognize a fear or a painful statement of your own, consider trying this exercise.

For example, if, like me, you are afraid that you won't be taken care of, ask, "Is it true that I won't be taken care of?" When you receive your answer, you can turn that into a question to check it out. So, if the first answer that comes to you is, *You will be taken care of,* and you are not sure that's true, ask, *Is it true that I will be taken care of?* I did this one time after receiving my tax bill.

For a few minutes after leaving my accountant's office, I was paralyzed by the fear that I would not be able to take care of myself financially.

I was worried that after I paid my taxes,
I would not have enough.

At that time, just a year out of graduate school, half my net income went toward the minimum payment on my educational loans. That was every other paycheck, and that invoked in me a lot of fear.

Because I had been learning how to heal my own painful beliefs, I did not allow the fear to dominate me that day as I had in the past. As soon as I began to feel overwhelmed, I paused, allowed myself to shed tears, and asked myself, *What is this really about?* The first thing that came to my mind was, *I'm afraid I won't be taken care of.* This was a familiar and recurring fear for me.

I felt my breath quickening and had an urge to run away. When I noticed those body sensations, I paused for a moment to orient to my surroundings. I looked around me, noticed as many details as possible, and then reminded myself that in that moment I was safe. The sensation of anxiety quieted, and I continued with the exercise.

My mind wanted to review all the times in the past when I had not felt taken care of, but I did not allow that. Nor did I allow my mind to dwell on the fear. Instead, I turned my fear into a question, closed my eyes, and asked, *Is it true that I won't be taken care of?* Immediately, I saw the answer in my mind's eye: *No, that isn't true.*

*I paused to allow my answer to sink in
by expanding my breathing
and allowing my body to express itself.*

My fearful crying turned into tears of relief and gratitude as a sense of peace washed over me. I let out a cleansing sigh and said out loud what my intuition told me was true, "Everything will be okay." All of this happened in about three minutes, inside my parked car.

I had gotten into my car overwhelmed by the feeling that this problem was huge and that it would take a long time to overcome it. That's what happens when our reactions are supported by a painful belief.

*The fear that I would not be taken care of
was supported by the beliefs:
"I am not quite enough," and "I have to do it all myself."*

The belief *I have to do it all myself* is common in layer two, and it's confusing for those who are in service, because even though it hurts us, it is rewarded. Think about it: how do people respond when you take care of others and do more?

If my coworkers and I were discussing a difficult, unpopular project, and I offered, "I'll take that project on," would they say, "Gosh, Annie, you shouldn't do that. You've already got enough on your plate"? Probably not. They'd probably say, "Wow, Annie's such a trooper. I love working with Annie because she never says no!" Responses like that feel good, and we can use them to justify our painful beliefs (such as, *I have do it all myself*).

Eventually we become weary of overextending ourselves
and easily blame others for our pain.

Do you know anybody who often volunteers to do more? Have you ever heard that person complaining about the people they're helping? They might say, "Sure, I'll do that," and then turn to a coworker or go home and say, "Can you believe they asked me to take over that project? Why doesn't anybody appreciate everything I do? Don't they realize how overworked and tired I am?" (Can you see how these reactions can happen at home, too?)

What if I volunteered to help my colleague, Patrick, and then I turned to a coworker and said, "Did you know that Patrick asked me to take on another project for him? Can you believe that? What does he do all day?" And what if I didn't speak to Patrick directly because I didn't believe it was okay for me to say no, and I really hate conflict?

Layer two is where gossip lives,
because in layer two we talk about people
rather than talking to them.

When we consider a problem from layer two, we see more work
for ourselves. Often, depending on how long we have lived in
this layer, we feel resentful when we see more work for ourselves,
and we still take it on. On the surface, it might seem like we
take on extra responsibilities because we care about others and
we want to help them. There's nothing wrong with that; helping
one another can be a beautiful expression of love. On the other
hand, helping others actually can be an expression of control,
driven by the fear that we are not enough and the belief that
we are right. In layer two, even though we want what the other
person wants, we still believe we are right.

Layer two feeds codependence for the same reason that it feeds
gossip. That is, when we are in layer two, we refuse to speak our
truth.

Rather than saying what we really want or need,
we say what we think other people want to hear,
or we tell people what to do.

We start to feel irritable and resentful, not because other people
won't do what they should, which is the first thing that occurs to

us, but because we are out of integrity with ourselves. Integrity means "wholeness."

*When we are honest about how we really feel
and what we really need or want, then, and only then,
we can experience wholeness.*

One summer, a friend of mine asked me to help her understand this idea that she could want what another person wanted but also believe that she was right. I had spent a long weekend at her home in the mountains, along with her family, her sister, and her sister's two dogs. That made four adults, two children, three dogs, and a cat under one roof for four days. In that time, my friend had run herself ragged trying to make sure everyone was happy.

When I pointed this out, she said, "Right, so what's wrong with that?"

I asked, "In the past few days, did you ever feel irritated that your kids or your husband weren't helping you, or they weren't doing what you wanted them to do?"

With a startled look, she said, "Well, yes, but that's because—"

I interrupted her with "You're right. Even though you want what they want, meaning you want them to be happy and have a good time, you also want them to do it the way that you know they should—the right way. Isn't that true?"

"Oh my gosh!" she declared. "That *is* true!"

*By considering her reactions and thoughts,
my friend saw a different side of herself
in the mirror of her experiences with her family.*

She realized that while she had been running around monitoring everyone else, she had not been fully present with any of us, so she felt dissatisfied with the weekend, and she felt unseen. She was frustrated that she had worked hard while her family had played. Even though her actions had been her own choice, she felt like she had no other options. She believed she had to do it all herself.

During my visit, my friend had really wanted some time alone with me, which I also had wanted. But until our last day, most of our time had been consumed by busyness. After our conversation, she told the others that she and I were going to spend thirty minutes alone.

She felt surprised and happy when nobody got upset or felt neglected. In fact, they were glad to give us some space. We enjoyed giving each other our full attention, and we ended my visit feeling seen, connected, nurtured, and deeply grateful for our friendship.

*When someone says even one word about how they feel,
that energy starts to release.*

We can then have a much better conversation about what the real problem is and how we can resolve it. In my friend's case, the problem was not that her family didn't help her around the house that weekend. The problem was that she believed she wasn't quite enough, so she pushed herself to keep busy and try to ensure everyone else's happiness. I used to do the same thing.

In the summer of 2003, I eagerly anticipated a new adventure: graduate school. Based on my experience with my master's program, I knew that I would be happier and more successful if I entered school as a full-time student. I was married at the time, and my husband fully supported my decision to quit my job and focus on school.

I had spent years preparing for my PhD program, planning how quickly I could complete it, finding just the right person to mentor me, and waiting until everything lined up perfectly. You see, I had always been the perfect planner.

*I lived by the layer-two belief, "I am not quite enough,"
so I took care to envision and carefully manage
every detail of my life.*

By early August, I felt confident and excited. After three years of waiting, my husband and I decided this would be the perfect time to start a family. Also, I had always loved being in school, and I had a feeling this program would change my life. I never expected my intuition would be so painfully accurate.

I arrived at work one morning, ready to give notice that I would be leaving. Before I had the chance, I was notified that my position would be eliminated as part of a reorganization.

Even though I had prepared myself to be unemployed, this notice inspired in me self-doubt. Even though I had been nominated for several company awards, I wondered if I had done something wrong to make my employer eliminate my position. And, even though I did not want to stay there, I felt a sense of loss.

Being the consummate optimist, I quickly turned from my emotions and focused on positive thoughts: graduate school and a long-yearned-for family of my own. Within days, I received a second, much more painful shock. My husband had been feeling very tired for months, and on my birthday, we found out why: he had cancer. Our plans flew out the window as he entered surgery four days later, on his birthday.

I had always been calm in a crisis, and this time was no different. I poured my energy into researching options and support groups for my husband, telling myself I would get my own support later.

*All communication focused on what to do
rather than on how we felt or what we needed.*

The truth is, I was thinking, *Here we go again. The bottom has dropped out from under me, just like it always does. I knew my dreams were not really for me. I just wish someone would hold me and tell me I'm not alone.* That's what I was thinking, but no one knew it.

Within a three-week period, I lost my job, my husband was diagnosed with cancer and began treatment, my hopes for pregnancy were dashed, and I entered a PhD program. I didn't know it yet, but my fierce attachment to personal strength and independence was about to crumble.

Rather than open up to my grief,
I turned on myself.

When I wasn't focused on my husband's needs, I directed my energy toward berating myself. I judged myself for waiting so long to start a family. I judged myself as arrogant for assuming I had plenty of time to wait. When I couldn't help it, I cried rivers of tears—alone.

I entered my PhD program exhausted but grateful for the structure it might provide. I so yearned for predictability and a positive reflection of my value that I registered for fifteen credits, even though my husband was ill, even though my life was in shambles. Why? Because that helped me to have a sense of control and generate evidence on which to assess my worth. I had always looked outside myself to gauge my worth, by getting good grades, taking care of other people, and putting on a happy face.

Soon, I became overwhelmed. I realized that I could not continue to ignore my heart. In desperation, I started working with Rebecca, a gifted counselor. Rebecca was the only person I allowed to see my neediness, because …

I believed my needs were unacceptable.

I couldn't be needy! I was the fix-it person! And besides, people usually left me when I was needy.

Well, my heart was broken, and I couldn't fix it, and I couldn't continue to deny it. I had to open to another way. One of the first principles Rebecca taught me was that life is a mirror of the core beliefs we hold about ourselves. She politely and gently held my heart as I slowly opened to what life was reflecting to me.

After I had settled into my school routine, I noticed that a certain woman appeared in four of my five classes. That was unusual in my doctoral program because students had a wide range of classes to choose from. It also was unusual that this woman made the hair on my neck stand up. I hated being near her, and I'm a very easygoing person! I'm usually calm and personable, and I get along with most people.

I could not stand for her to be in the same room with me. I cringed when she opened her mouth to speak; her voice aggravated me every time I heard it. When I thought about how strongly this woman triggered me, I realized that ...

There may have been something inside me that was causing my reaction to my classmate. Maybe she was a mirror for me.

Because I was such a good student (and because I still believed I had to do everything myself), I spent three months trying to figure out what was being reflected to me. Three months! Every day, I spent time observing my reactions to my classmate, observing my judgments of her, and asking myself, *How is she a mirror for me?*

Finally, I went to Rebecca and said, "I need some help, because I can't figure it out, and I really would like this to end."

Rebecca replied, "Okay, tell me about this woman."

I said, "Well, she's never prepared. She always has an excuse. She presents herself as a victim, and she doesn't really have that many bright ideas to share." I was completely honest!

Rebecca asked, "How do the faculty respond?"

I replied, "It's really crazy. They always give her another chance, and they don't seem to hold her accountable. They always help her out." And that made me even madder, because I was on time, prepared, with everything done, while she got more chances.

This is why it was hard for me to see the reflection. I had been looking for evidence that I was not doing enough, but I couldn't think of anything else I could be doing. That day, I learned that …

The reflections life offers are to support our healing,
not to increase our suffering.

When I was finished with my description, Rebecca said, "It sounds like she's receiving a lot of compassion." Never in a million years would I have come to that conclusion, but I had to admit that it was true; she was being given a lot of compassion.

When I acknowledged this, Rebecca asked, "Annie, what would it be like if you allowed yourself to ask for help and receive compassion like that?" As soon as that question hit my ears, I burst into tears. In the space of one second, I went from talking calmly to sobbing, because I couldn't even imagine what Rebecca was suggesting—that I was worthy of asking for and receiving help.

While I cried, a movie played in my mind of many experiences from my life that had reinforced the beliefs that it was not okay for me to ask for help, and that I needed to be able to do it all myself. I did not stop with any of the pictures. I just watched them pass by and stayed focused on my heart.

Giving myself permission to release my emotions gave me so much relief. It also opened up the willingness to make a new choice. I said to myself, *I choose to believe that it might be possible that it might be okay for me to ask for help.*

All of this is about incremental, baby steps. Remember, be gentle and go slowly. I did not immediately feel confident or comfortable asking for help, but I did feel less overwhelmed by everything that was on my plate, and ...

I began to trust that help was available.

I continued to work with Rebecca, and my husband made a full recovery. Although we later ended our marriage, the decision arose out of deep respect for each other. With Rebecca's help, we were able to move out of reaction and make the transition in a thoughtful, loving way.

As I explained earlier, at least two benefits come when we look for what life is mirroring and turn toward our part. The first is that we grow. The second is that the source of the reflection goes away or softens. In my example from graduate school, the source went away. In the following three years, I saw that classmate only a few times.

When I saw her, I spontaneously felt
compassion for her, which surprised me.

When I thought about her, my initial reaction—which in the past had involved my stomach clenching and my mind generating judgmental thoughts—changed to compassion. I did not try to make that happen, but I was really glad that it did.

If I had interacted with her, I am certain it would have been a lot easier for me. I would have been able to be present with her, rather than with my judgments of myself, which she was reflecting back to me. I did not try to change my feelings about or judgments of her.

I changed my judgments of myself,
and that changed how I saw everyone else.

If you find that a particular personality really drives you crazy, or a particular situation causes you pain and seems to repeat itself, look for the reflection. It's really helpful to remember that those people and situations are simply mirroring our core beliefs about ourselves.

*When we are upset, it is never about the other person.
It is always about something deeper in ourselves.*

It might not seem like it now, but it is far easier to change a belief or an agreement than it is to force ourselves to act differently while holding onto what is causing the pain. That's because when we change our beliefs, our actions change naturally.

What to Do When Someone Else Is in Layer Two

When your friend is in layer two, he or she is yearning for acceptance and support. Remember that if you feel frustrated. If you want to help yourself, ask yourself how your friend is a mirror for you. If you want to help your friend, you might ask how you can support him or her, or you might take a moment to tell your friend how much he or she means to you.

If the friend cringes or tries to change the subject, you can gently and politely tell him or her that you mean what you say, and ask your friend to pause and really listen to you. Then tell your friend again how much he or she means to you, and give specific examples of why.

You won't be able to make your loved ones receive your words. That's not your job. Instead, you might call their attention to their reaction to your words. You might say, "I noticed that you cringed when I said I admire you. Can you help me understand why?"

*Before you ask, make sure you are sincerely interested
in learning from their response.*

If you want to ask the question in order to teach your loved ones something or give them advice, it's best not to ask, because that effort to control will likely spark a new reaction. In that case, do your best to help yourself move through your own reaction and let your loved ones be responsible for themselves.

If you want to help someone who gives you unsolicited advice or constantly tells you what to do, set a boundary. Healthy boundaries are incredibly supportive of positive communication. Before you begin, you might review the tips for setting clear boundaries at the end of the previous chapter.

Tips for Moving through Layer Two

Be curious about your thoughts, emotions, body sensations, and intuition.

Set aside five minutes, as often as you can, just to notice what's going on in each of your organs of perception. Turn off your phone and other electronics, settle into your favorite chair, and gently close your eyes. Begin with whatever catches your attention.

You might notice a part of your body that feels tight or an emotion even before you notice what's going on in your mind. Be curious about what you notice; pay attention to as many details as you can. Try to avoid deciding whether your experience is good or bad or trying to change it. The more you can become familiar with the various ways your mind, heart, body, and spirit/intuition communicate, the easier it will be to move through layers one and two.

Notice when you blame other people or events for your situation or mood.

That's a sign that you have given your power away. Instead of focusing your attention on anything outside of yourself, ask yourself what you need, what you fear, what you feel, how your body feels—questions that will help you move out of your head and open your heart.

Be aware of giving unsolicited advice (which includes backseat driving, darn it).

If you find yourself telling people what to do, see if you can identify the fear that is behind your urge to control. For example, parents might try to control their child who is recovering from an addiction because they fear a relapse. I might try to tell my husband how to drive because I fear being late. Our fears come from a place inside ourselves, so they can only be resolved if we turn our attention inward, rather than trying to control other people or events.

Remember that everyone is on his or her own journey through life.

The suffering you want to spare him could be just what he needs to grow. The pleasure you are certain she would experience if she just took your advice might not be what she wants right now.

Remember that other people might have preferences, needs, and priorities that are different from yours.

Can you give them space to be who they are? Can you give yourself space to be who you really are?

Write down what you want to experience in your thoughts, your body sensations, your emotions, and your connection to your intuition and spirit.

If you already have a list or vision board of what you want to have, you can add to that. If you don't have such a list, there is no need to build one. Ask yourself, "If I were to get what I want, how would that change my experience?" Notice how envisioning what you want to experience is the same as or different from envisioning what you want.

Maintain a gratitude journal.

I find this very helpful for refreshing my hope and lightening my heart.

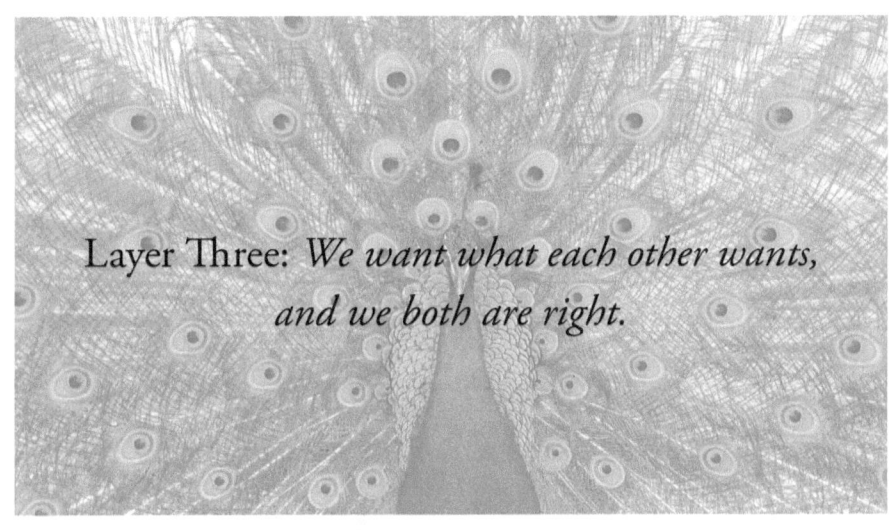

Layer Three: *We want what each other wants,
and we both are right.*

My core belief is:
I am enough right now.

My mind tells me:
We are equally worthy of _____.
There is enough _____ for me.
We are not in competition.

I feel:
Open
Safe
Connected

I project onto you:
I want you to have what you want.

When I consider a conflict from layer three,
I see:
My part; how I contribute to the problem
And I:
Dialogue with you

When I communicate from layer three, you might think that I want what you want, and I want what I want. That means that both are possible at the same time; we are not in competition.

If we're both in layer three, we want what each other wants. I might ask myself, *What is it that he wants that I can want for him?* rather than asking a layer-one question like, *What can I get from him?* or a layer-two question like, *What can I do for him?*

In layer three, I am more open to the information coming from my heart, my body, and my spirit. This enables me to recognize painful beliefs more quickly, so I can move through them more quickly.

How great would it be in negotiations (in business and at home) if both of us could be open and sincerely want what each other wants? It's an exchange of support. It is not, "I'm going to do for you and never receive anything in return," (layer two) or, "You should do more for me," (layer one).

The core belief in layer three is, *I am enough, right now.* Right now, in this moment, with this body and these needs and these emotions, I am enough. When we are able to connect to that truth and let it permeate our hearts and bodies, then our minds tell us that we are equally worthy.

We can rest in the full knowledge that
there is enough for everyone,
so we need not be in competition
for love, power, money, or stuff.

A few years ago, I spent a day and a half coaching a couple who owned a business together and had reached an impasse in their communication. When we started, they were blaming each other for their unhappiness at work. Each had plenty of good reasons as to why the other was responsible for the problems in their business.

Her complaints about him included, "He leaves whenever he wants. I never know what's going on, and then I feel like an idiot because if a customer comes in to check on their job, I can't answer their questions."

His complaints were, "She's too controlling. She always wants to know where I am, and I didn't go into business to be controlled. I want to be able to take a break during the day and do something fun once in a while."

So, they were not in layer three at the beginning of our time together. They were in layer one: *I want what I want, and I am right.* "I want to be able to leave whenever I want to!" he'd shout. "Well, I want to be able to answer customers' questions and have accurate records!" she'd shout back.

At one point, I asked them to think about why they were in business. If the business ran itself, what would they get out of owning it? I wrote their responses side-by-side on a white board, and when they were finished, I asked them to take a moment to read what was on the board. Then, I asked what they noticed about the lists. After a minute or two, the husband said, "They're the same."

I said, "Exactly."

❧

At the core, they wanted the same thing: freedom.

❧

The way they experienced that freedom was different. He experienced freedom by knowing that he could leave whenever he wanted to, and when he came back his business would still be running. She experienced freedom in having all the information she needed, and knowing that she would be able to confidently answer customers' questions.

After we came to this awareness, tension released, and she said to him, "You know, I don't really mind if you leave when you want. I actually want that for you. I want you to have that freedom. We've spent ten years building this business, and I want you to be free to enjoy yourself."

I asked him, "Can you see how you can support your wife's freedom by giving her the information she needs before you leave? And then your freedom will expand?"

He said, "Wow, yes, I can." Suddenly, it was no problem for him to give her information. It was easy for him, because …

He understood that her requests were intended to support her freedom, not to limit his.

In this layer, you can ask yourself, *What do they want that I can want for them?* Let's say you are hiring a new employee, and they want more money. Maybe you can't give them more money because of your budget, but what does money symbolize? Security is one thing. Self-worth is another. Money is loaded with emotional charge.

You could ask yourself, *What is it that this person really wants?* and go with your gut instinct (or better yet, ask them directly).

If you get the sense that they really want security and they think that more money would give it to them, ask yourself what you could offer them that would help them experience more security. Is there an opportunity for growth with the company that you can outline for them? Is there an opportunity for the position to have more influence?

New possibilities enter our awareness
when we free ourselves from the surface.

The surface in the example above is money. Money discussions are rarely about money. Usually, they are driven by something deeper like a desire for security, authority, or self-worth.

If you can identify the deeper desire,
then you also will be able to identify
alternative, satisfactory solutions.

At the beginning of our session, my business-owner clients felt disconnected from each other, and each believed that the other made their job miserable. They had been considering not working together (which would have cost them a lot more money and limited their freedom). They were feeling separated, and they were focused on blame.

When we finished our time together, those dear people told me they felt seen, heard, and hopeful. I was happy that layer three had helped them open to information from their deeper thoughts, feelings, and body sensations, and, ultimately, to love.

In layer three, our communication with others becomes more balanced. We allow a full range of emotions and opinions to be expressed, without trying to manage or change them. We remain present in the current moment rather than having one foot in the past and one in the future.

In layer three, we can see how we contribute
to every situation we find ourselves in,
and we are open to learning what others want
without removing their self-responsibility.

That's why it is possible to reach new, healthy agreements when we are in layer three. In layer one, I see only your part; I think you are responsible for everything. In layer two, I see only my part; I think I am responsible for fixing everything. In layer three, I recognize how I contribute to a problem, and I am open to learning how you feel and what you want. I feel safe to talk with you, so it becomes possible for us to reach a resolution together.

I shared this with my friend, Ann, when she called me at the beginning of a road trip from California to Montana. Her travel companion had just told her that she wanted to explore western California because this would be her last visit to the area.

Ann wanted to make some progress toward Montana, but she had not said anything because she did not want to deny her friend her "last chance to see western California." She wasn't sure what to do.

I pointed out something that was obvious to me, since I was focused on the present, but might have seemed naive to Ann's friend, who was focused on the future. I said, "What you know for sure is that you're in western California right now. That's all you know.

"Your friend might believe that she will never return to the area, when in fact she could get a call next week that will bring her back. Who knows? I don't. But what I do know is …"

*Any time I make a decision based on
a limiting belief or an attempt to control
someone else's experience, it feels yucky.*

Ann decided to be honest about her preference to get on the road and to let her friend be responsible for herself. Eventually, both of them reached layer three. They were able to be present, hear what each other wanted, and reach an agreement that felt good to both of them.

You might not realize it, but every relationship we are in functions by agreement. Many of these agreements have never been spoken. We get into habits and patterns that become so familiar we might think, *This is just the way it is; it'll never change.* In fact, every relationship, especially our relationship to ourselves, can change.

Usually, it is easier to see agreements in relationships that feel good. For example, I'm guessing that it makes sense to say that if you and a friend comfort each other or celebrate each other's accomplishments, you have agreed to do that. However, it also is true that if you bicker, you have agreed to bicker.

*It is difficult to recognize a painful agreement
when we think the other person is to blame.*

Remember the reaction cycle that happens in layer one of communication: *I observe something or interact with someone ... I dwell on what happened ... I experience a reaction ... I wait for it to happen again ... I observe something or interact with someone ...* Reaction often includes blame, which reinforces a perception that the other person has the power, and that reinforces reaction. This happens quite often in healthcare when nurses and other staff believe they cannot speak up to a physician.

I have coached many nurses who were fearful of speaking up. Each time, I found the reaction cycle constricting their ability to speak their truth and challenge authority, even when patients' safety was at risk. It looked like this: *I saw the doctor yell at my coworker after she was reminded to wash her hands ... I dwelled on what happened ... I felt anger and irritation toward the doctor and wondered when my manager would do something about doctors yelling at nurses ... I dreaded that doctor yelling again and did my best to stay out of her way.*

The culture of medicine has reinforced for generations the belief that physicians should not be challenged, and that belief has harmed patients. Just as the airline industry supports copilots speaking up when they think something is wrong, leaders in healthcare are working to open up communication between physicians and their non-MD titled colleagues. Why? Because everyone involved with healthcare wants the same thing: to help patients be well.

I have never met a physician who wanted to harm patients by not listening to nurses. The doctors I have worked with told me they felt personally responsible for their patients' outcomes, pressured to have the right answers, and rushed by the pace of their department or clinic.

They wanted to experience healthier, more positive interactions with their colleagues, but they did not know how to change their communication habits.

Sound familiar? Whether you work in your home, a small family business, or an intense public industry like healthcare, you probably can relate to one or more of the pressures doctors face. Everyone confronts the reaction cycle now and then. As I tell nurses and other clients: the fact is, if another person treats you like a doormat, you have agreed to allow that to happen.

The key to breaking the cycle is to develop awareness of what is below the surface inside of ourselves, rather than give our power away by blaming someone for our situation.

That doesn't mean that you deserve to be treated like a doormat. You don't. Ever. But you should know that such treatment is evidence of an agreement. One of my clients, Lisa, learned this when she bitterly complained to me that she had been underpaid for a job she had done.

Lisa appeared frail because she was extremely thin with sparse, white hair, hunched shoulders, and fair skin marked with sores. Slumped in her chair with tears in her eyes, Lisa whimpered, "My boss intimidated me into claiming fewer hours than I actually worked. He's such a jerk!"

Lisa believed that her boss was
to blame for her situation
because he had intimidated her.

Even though she was in her midsixties, when Lisa said her boss had intimidated her, she looked and sounded just like a frail little girl. As she continued to explain her situation, she described what her boss had done over the years to demean and undervalue her. While Lisa spoke, I could see that she was in pain mentally, physically, and emotionally. After all, if it were true that she was a victim of her boss's behavior, then she was powerless.

Lisa's belief in her helplessness
had drained the vitality from her body.

I invited Lisa to pause for a moment, take a few full breaths, and focus her attention on the room we were in (to help her return to the present moment). Then I suggested, "Let's not give him any more attention. Instead, let's see if this situation feels familiar. Can you think of other times when you felt like someone took advantage of you, or is this problem with your boss the first time?"

*It can be helpful to notice patterns
because they reveal our underlying agreements and beliefs.*

Lisa sat back in her chair, thought for a moment, and then said, "Actually, every boss I've ever had has treated me this way. I'm sick of it."

"Good!" I replied. "I think you're ready to own your power."

"My what?" she asked, with a startled look on her face.

"Your power, Lisa," I said. "You have the power to change your relationship with your boss, regardless of whether or not he changes his behavior toward you."

At first, Lisa was frustrated that I would not join her in blaming her boss. The more we talked about it, however, the more Lisa recognized that she had silently agreed to be a doormat for her boss. He had criticized her work since the day she joined his staff, more than twelve years before. He had never thanked her for her efforts or acknowledged the value she brought to his department. Yet, Lisa had stayed. She had remained silent toward her boss and then dwelled on what happened, telling the story over and over, thereby increasing her resentment and reinforcing her belief that she was powerless.

Whenever you see yourself as a victim,
it is a sign that you have given your power away.

I explained, "Every challenging relationship will get worse, until you own your part and your power. It sounds like not being paid for your work is the last straw. What do you think? Are you ready to change your agreement with your boss?"

"Well, I don't know," Lisa hesitantly replied. "I'm scared of his reaction."

"I can understand," I said, because …

When we are accustomed to silencing ourselves
in order to keep the peace, it can feel scary
to speak our truth and allow space
for the other person to have his or her own feelings.

"Just remember that no one can prevent you from changing an agreement. Your part belongs to you. It is not your job to keep your boss happy or to protect him from the consequences of his dishonest actions."

"You're right!" Lisa declared, her big, green eyes suddenly alive. "I'm ready." Her face had regained its color. She looked like a grown woman when she confidently asked, "How do I do it?" In reply, I guided Lisa through the process for reaching new agreements described below.

That day, Lisa shifted her attention from her boss to herself. Rather than giving her power away (by seeing herself as a victim of her boss's behavior), Lisa opened up to the possibility that she could avoid further harm by changing what she had the power to change: her own behavior. The following week, Lisa turned in her resignation, reported her boss to the company's compliance officer, and unexpectedly was offered a better job—all in the same day!

How to Reach New Agreements

In the example below, I have included a simple description of how this process might be used in a hospital to resolve a common point of contention among nurses: break times. It's also very useful for managers who want to coach employees toward improved performance. The language I use in the example might seem overly formal; if you use this guide to prepare for your own conversation, use words that feel natural to you.

Preparing for the Conversation

Before you speak to the other person, answer the two questions below. The way you bring yourself to the conversation will have a big impact on how well you and the other person communicate with each other because the other person will reflect back to you the degree to which you are open to them.

Am I in Reaction?

- If you speak from reaction, you will get more reaction in return. The tips for moving through reaction, listed in the chapter on layer one, can help you to prepare.

- If you pause to allow your reaction to soften and remind yourself of what you want out of the conversation, you will be much more likely to communicate positively.

What is my intention?
- If your intention is to prove to someone that he or she is wrong, keep in mind that your conversation will just be an exchange of reactions.
- If your intention is to be understood, keep in mind that you cannot control whether or not another person understands you. You might, instead, hold the intention to respectfully and clearly speak your truth. That is something you have full control over.
- If your intention is to clarify expectations and reach a new agreement, state that when you ask the other person to talk with you. Most people will be more open to a conversation about expectations and agreements because that implies that they will have an equal share in the conversation.

Having the Conversation: Observation—Impact—Request

To open, state your intention and ask if the other person agrees to it. This will help the other person focus on your words rather than being distracted by assumptions about why you want to talk. For example, a nurse might say to a coworker, "I'd like to talk with you about our agreement regarding breaks. Is that all right with you?" (Nurses, especially those who work in busy hospitals, often miss their breaks in order to take care of patients or due to coworkers being late. Nurses who repeatedly miss their breaks can become resentful of those who take breaks.)

Stating your intention is a good way to check your motives. Imagine saying to someone, "I'd like to talk with you so I can prove that you were wrong. Would that be all right with you?" It's easy to imagine what kind of response you're likely to get!

Remember that the other person will have his or her own observations, needs, and opinions and might be in reaction at times during your conversation. Do your best to allow space for the other person to share, without trying to change or "fix" his or her thoughts or feelings. Even though you want something from that person, you might try to listen from the position of, *What does he want that I can want for him?* That can help you find common ground.

OBSERVATION

DESCRIBE THE ACTIONS AND WORDS YOU DIRECTLY OBSERVED.

Avoid speaking for other people by referring to what others have said or what others think. Unless it's followed by a compliment, most of us become defensive when we hear, "Everyone says that you ..." Stay focused on your direct experience and be specific. What did you observe? When did it occur?

REMEMBER THAT THERE IS A BIG DIFFERENCE BETWEEN OBSERVATION AND INTERPRETATION.

It's easy to think that our interpretations are factual because our minds so quickly interpret everything we observe. Here are two tips for recognizing which is which:

- Observations include unarguable facts. For example, "At 3:00, I went to look for you and found you in the break room, even though your break was scheduled to end at 2:45."

- Interpretations include generalizations or judgments. For example, "You're never where you're supposed to be," or, "You must not care about how much work the rest of us have, since you take such long breaks."

IMPACT

STAY FOCUSED ON YOUR EXPERIENCE AND BE SPECIFIC.

How was your work or your customer affected? Or, if you are not speaking about work, how were you personally affected? If you were not directly affected, then the issue might not be any of your business. Ask yourself if you might be overstepping the boundaries between yourself and someone else or taking responsibility for something that actually belongs to someone else.

HOW DID/DO YOU FEEL ABOUT IT?

To describe your feelings, begin with, "When that happened, I felt …" Avoid saying, "You made me feel," or, "It made me feel." Nothing can "make" you feel a certain way. If you use those phrases, you will give your power away, and the other person will likely become defensive or focus on shame, neither of which will be helpful.

For example, "When I had to look for you, it impacted my work by taking up time that I could have spent with our patients. When that happened, I felt frustrated and angry, because I want to spend as much time with patients as possible."

KEEP IN MIND THAT YOU PROBABLY DO NOT HAVE ALL THE INFORMATION.

Invite the other person to share. "Help me understand" is a very useful phrase. For example: "Help me understand why you were in the break room at 3:00." You might also phrase it as a question: "Can you help me understand why you were in the break room at 3:00?"

Of course, the way you say it will affect how it is received, but if you really do want to know, the other person will be less defensive than if you skipped this step. And, you might learn some important information. Perhaps your coworker was late in beginning her break.

REQUEST

It is one thing to express what you observed and how it impacted you. If the other person quickly apologizes, and you feel better, it can be easy to end the conversation without making a request. However, if you stop there, you and the other person will have to assume what you want, and you won't have a clear agreement. That is always a setup for disappointment, for both of you.

IF YOU DID NOT LIKE WHAT YOU OBSERVED, WHAT WOULD YOU PREFER?

Be clear and specific. For example: "Next time, would you please come back from your break on time?" If she had begun her break late, you might say, "Next time, if you can't leave for your break on time, would you please correct the schedule or tell me before you leave? That way, I will know when to expect you back and can prepare for my own break."

Some people believe a conversation like the example I've just given should occur only between a manager and her employee. Many times, I have heard angry employees say, "It isn't my job to talk to my coworkers about what they should or shouldn't do!"

That is just an excuse for not speaking their truth; it reinforces a false belief that they are victims.

Regardless of organizational politics,
I have always found that relationships improved faster
when people spoke directly to each other.

CLOSE

THANK THEM FOR TALKING WITH YOU.
You might restate your agreement to make sure you heard each other. For example: "Thanks for talking with me today. Before we close, I'd like to make sure I've got it. We agree that … Is that right?" That step is particularly helpful if you have agreed to multiple steps or you are not sure if you heard the other person accurately.

It isn't always necessary to speak to someone
in order to change your agreement with them.

If you aren't going to maintain a relationship with the other person, there really is no reason why you must involve them in crafting your new agreement. Remember Lisa? She changed her agreement with her former boss without inviting his input.

She had no desire to maintain a relationship with him, so it was unnecessary for her to reach an agreement with him. Instead, her decision to respect herself and own her power became a boundary she set with her boss (i.e., she quit).

Remember my clients who owned a business together? They reached a new agreement to share information. They agreed to meet daily for ten minutes to update each other on clients and projects. He agreed to use an "In/Out" board to let everyone in their business know when he would be back if he stepped out during the day. She agreed to show him how to use their electronic filing system so he could access files when she was out of the office.

These agreements were only possible after they had realized what each other wanted below the surface: freedom. If we had skipped the steps that revealed what they really wanted, instead spending all our time discussing tasks (like why he "should" use an In/Out board), there would have been too much resistance to make any lasting progress.

When we identified what was behind the desire for information, the couple was able to reach agreements that supported both of them. They opened up to their love for each other and saw that they sincerely wanted what each other wanted.

Both of them could be right at the same time
because there was no need for one to lose
in order for the other to get what he/she wanted.

That's what is possible in layer three of communication—unity. It takes practice to go below the surface, but it is *so* worth it. Layer three is a great place to be! Every relationship becomes easier when we communicate from the heart, especially relationships with children.

During my late twenties and early thirties, my best girlfriends welcomed children into their lives while I moved all over the country pursuing my career and personal healing. On visits home, I was glad to hear little ones call me "Aunt Annie," but I also felt a lingering sadness about not having children of my own.

When I would visit a friend's home, the first thing I'd do is hug my girlfriend, and then I would disappear with one or more kids as they showed me all the new discoveries and crafts they'd made since my last visit. Nothing felt better to me than seeing their eyes shine with pride as I cooed over their dolls, Legos, and wondrous creations.

One day during a long visit, I noticed that Rafe, who was two, left the room every time I entered, and when I called to him, he ran away. I really wanted him to cuddle with me, and I couldn't understand why he suddenly didn't want anything to do with me. At first I felt hurt, rejected. Then I thought about all the possible "logical" explanations for his change in behavior toward me. However, logic really isn't relevant when dealing with a two-year-old, so I quickly abandoned that endeavor.

Finally, I decided to shift my attention from what Rafe was doing to what I was doing. *How am I bringing myself to Rafe?* I wondered. *Am I offering love to him, or am I asking him to offer it to me?*

I had to admit that while I was offering love to Rafe, I also wanted him to give me attention. I felt empty, and I wanted him to distract me from that emptiness.

*Without words, Rafe was teaching me that
my silent yearning communicated loudly.*

Like many toddlers, he could tell the difference between when I approached him with an unspoken expectation (that he cuddle with me or smile at me) and when I came to him feeling complete within myself, having no expectations of him.

I decided to do an experiment, to see if I was right that Rafe could tell whether or not I wanted something from him. First, I took responsibility for my own feelings and reminded myself that Rafe was two; it was not his job to make me feel better. Then, every time I saw Rafe or thought about him, I imagined myself saying to him, "You are perfect, just as you are. I don't want anything from you."

Rafe kept his distance for the first day. The second day, I noticed him watching me, still from a distance, but now exchanging smiles and giggles with me. By the third day, there was no residue left of my desire for Rafe to give me his attention. In fact, I nearly forgot about the whole thing.

*I focused on being fully present,
no matter what I was doing or who I was with.*

Around three that afternoon, I was talking about Halloween costumes with Rafe's big sisters, Olivia and Amelia, when suddenly Rafe climbed into my lap. He didn't say anything or even look at me. He just climbed up and turned around to face Olivia. I hadn't thought anyone else had noticed Rafe avoiding me, but as soon as Rafe climbed into my lap, Olivia exclaimed, "Hey, he likes you again!" So much communication, so few words.

Layer Four: *I want what is in the highest good for all living things, and love is right.*

You think you are a small star, when in fact, you contain the whole universe.[12]
~Sidi Shaykh Muhammad al-Jamal

My core belief is:
I am.

My mind tells me:
There is no such thing as enough/not enough.

I feel:
Hopeful
Content
Integrated

I project onto you:
Love

When I consider a conflict from layer four,
I see:
Alternatives
Connections
Possibilities

And I:
Am with you.
Make space for you.

When we communicate from layers one and two, we are primarily paying attention to our thoughts. In layer two, we start to notice body sensations. In layer three, we listen to our emotions, and in layer four, we connect to our spirits (which you also could call intuition, if that feels better to you). In layer four, we notice information from all of our organs of perception.

Perception expands in layer four.

On our way to layer four, we have shifted from being concerned primarily about ourselves (layer one), to collaborating with and supporting another person (layer three), to considering all living things. In this layer, we are free from the illusion that we are powerless. We remember that we are valuable and powerful, so we carefully consider the possible ripple effect of our words and actions.

Layer four is interesting because it doesn't necessarily include a lot of words. Have you ever soaked in a hot tub and then crawled into bed right after? Maybe you felt completely relaxed, and if somebody wanted to talk to you, your response was "Unh" or another sound that told them there was no way your brain was going to engage because you were so wonderfully nestled under the covers. That's kind of what layer four feels like to me: a sense of being completely connected to myself, relaxed, open, and safe.

When I am in layer four, if I ask for guidance about a problem or concern, I get a lot of insight. The movie that plays in my mind after I ask for guidance is totally different from the movie that plays in my mind when I'm in layer one. In just a minute, I will guide you through a practice that can help you experience layer four.

I tried to think of what my mind tells me in layer four, but it was hard because there isn't a lot of mental chatter when I'm in this layer. For me, the only thing on my mind is, "I am." This is very different from the other layers because there are no categories, titles, labels, or other adjectives. I just am.

In July 2008, I drove into Yellowstone National Park for the first time in ten years. Many significant events of my life had happened in Yellowstone, and I often yearned to be in nature, so it was a strong experience for me. As I drove, it occurred to me that I was, in that moment, being who I am.

I was not caught up in who others said I should be, what advertisers said I should look like, or who I'd thought I would become when I was little. Instead, I caught a glimpse of the endless love and light within me. In that moment, I was totally in alignment with who I am at my core—love, innocence, joy, complete unity. This realization opened a flood of cleansing tears. I pulled over to the side of the road along the river, allowed my tears to continue flowing, and wrote down my thoughts …

I feel such gratitude to be
reconnecting to who I am,
free from what the world thinks I should be,
who other people say I am, and
how the voices in my head tell me I should be. This is who I am:

I am a passionate woman
Who loves to love
And be loved.

Who knows the voice
Of nature
And settles easily
Into her embrace.

I am like
The vibrant wildflowers
That now
Surround me,

Blossoms
Whose beauty
Emerged
After
Intense fire,
Then
Healing
Water and light.

I am
That
Healing
Water and light.

That's who I am!

Healing
Water and light.

Everything else
Is
Illusion.

That journal entry is a good example of my awareness of the present moment when I am in layer four. In the other layers, my awareness of the present moment is fleeting and sporadic because my mind is busy with thoughts and worries. Layer four is rejuvenating because I am not worried about five minutes ago or five minutes from now. I am completely here in the moment— mind, body, heart, and spirit. I am. I don't have to qualify, judge, or categorize anything. It all just is.

In this layer, my mind tells me there really is no such thing as "enough" and "not enough."

I feel hopeful. I feel content, and I feel integrated. Rather than feeling alone, separated, or disoriented, in this layer I know that my emotions are okay, my thoughts are okay, my body sensations support me, my intuition is reliable, and I don't need to change anything.

If you and I talk about a problem, and I am in layer four, I project love onto you. You may not know that I'm projecting love, but you might feel comfortable or safe talking to me, even if your opinion or preference is different from mine. You might feel like you can be honest and say how you really feel because I am going to accept and make space for you.

When I consider a problem from layer four, I see connections, alternatives, and possibilities. I am with you, meaning that I make space for you to have your own opinions, emotions, and needs without making them wrong or trying to fix them for you. You don't have to agree with me because I don't have to be right.

Layer four enhances every relationship:
with ourselves, with nature,
with divine support, and with other people.

The layers of communication are just as relevant in business as in our personal lives. Can you imagine how useful it would be to cultivate layer four in your organization? Let's consider an information technology (IT) department, for example, that has a relationship with every other department. If your IT department were going to change e-mail programs, how would that affect them?

It would affect their workloads, their budget, and probably their work schedules as they dealt with more complexity. Wouldn't it be easy for staff in IT to be focused on how this new program would impact them? That would make sense. But, if they were in layer four, they also would consider how it might impact the users of e-mail in the organization. They might wonder, *How can we make the transition smooth for everyone?*

When we consider an organizational change from layer four,
we want what is in the highest good, and we are able to achieve it
because we see how all departments are connected.

When we witness these connections, we can anticipate the possibilities and the potential hurdles much more thoroughly. Speaking from personal experience, it feels a lot better to anticipate and communicate in advance than to try to pick up the pieces as more people (who, by the way, are in layer one) are calling and screaming because something's gone wrong, and they want it fixed *right now.*

There is freedom in the four layers of communication:
our choice to be in any particular layer is
independent of what other people choose for themselves.

With intention and practice, you can experience layer four, even if everyone around you is in reaction. It's really nice when other people are in layer four, and I know that I can be in layer four even if you are in layer one. One reason I can do that is that I understand how hard it is to change our core beliefs, so ...

Instead of judging or trying to change someone's state,
I can extend compassion toward them.

We cultivate our beliefs about ourselves from the time we're in the crib. Children look at the adults in their lives to decide: *Am I good? Am I bad? Is it okay for me to ask for what I need? Am I worthy of attention and love? Will I be taken care of? Can I relax?* It is understandable that we enter adulthood with painful beliefs about our worthiness and enoughness.

I feel lots of compassion for others (and myself) when I am in layer four. I acknowledge that I have no idea what others have experienced in life that generated or reinforced their painful core beliefs.

As soon as we recognize a painful belief,
we can pause to connect to layer four
and the guidance that is always available.

There is great hope in the awareness that we can stop suffering and start healing *right now*. I invite you to try a practice that can open your mind, body, heart, and spirit to this guidance. It doesn't matter if you have never done it before or if you have done something similar; this practice will support you. I learned it from the Shadhiliyya Sufis. It's called Remembrance.

Remembrance

During this practice, we are remembering that divine support is near and that we are much more than the labels, expectations, and fears that surround us. It is not necessary to follow any particular spiritual tradition or even to think of yourself as a spiritual being in order to benefit from Remembrance.

Remembrance is a practice that expands our openness to love, divine support, and our deep self, what some call our "higher self." I'm going to show you how Remembrance may be done as a way to gain insight regarding a concern. It also can be used when you simply want to relax deeply and increase your sense of being loved and supported.

First, make sure you are comfortable, either sitting or lying down. If you are sitting, you might put one or both feet on the floor, if that feels safe to you. You might put your hand on the center of your chest to help guide your attention to your heart and allow your mind to relax.

Take a gentle, deep breath. Let it out with a comfortable sigh. Cast your eyes down so you won't be distracted, or close your eyes. Now, bring to your awareness a concern or question. Imagine that problem or concern as a movie, playing right in front of you. Once you have a clear vision of the details of the concern …

Allow yourself to notice how the concern affects
your emotions, your body sensations, and your thoughts.

There is no need to dwell on it; just give yourself a chance to experience the impact of this concern. Then, imagine that the sun is shining from behind the image of your concern, toward you. Between you and the sun is the picture of your problem or concern.

For the next five breaths, let all of your attention be focused on the sunshine coming toward you, shining through your concern. You don't need to analyze or decide or change anything. Just experience what it's like to have warm, nurturing sunshine bathing your concern and you.

Imagine the warmth and light of the sunshine
embracing your body and filling every cell within you.

If thoughts come to your mind, that's okay. They will still be there when you're finished, so for now, give yourself permission to focus on the sunshine instead. Simply allow thoughts to flow freely in and out of your awareness, without stopping to analyze or listen to them.

After five breaths, pause and notice what that was like for you. How you are feeling? Are you aware of new or different thoughts? What do you notice about the way it feels to be in your body? Has anything changed? Don't worry if you feel no different or even worse; it might take time for you to trust yourself enough to open. Be kind to yourself by doing your best to continue, without trying to make something happen.

To deepen this practice, it can be very helpful to
repeat, either silently or aloud,
the name of God that feels best to you.

If there is no name of God that feels good to you, repeat the word Love, or Hope, or whatever you feel that your heart needs in the moment. Let's practice that for the next five to ten breaths. Picture your concern in front of you and the sun shining through your concern toward you.

Breathe at a relaxed, comfortable pace.
On each exhale, gently speak
the name of God or word that feels best to you.

Allow your attention to be focused on the sunshine and the name or word. Just as before, your mind can relax; you won't be asked to make any decisions or change anything for at least the next five to ten breaths.

When you are finished, very, very slowly open your eyes. In your journal or another private place, you might want to write down what you just experienced. What was that like for you? Did you get some new information? What is different now from when you first envisioned your problem or concern? Write down whatever you want to note for yourself.

Once, after I taught Remembrance to a group of human resource professionals, I asked what the experience had been like for them. One woman said, "My problem that I wrote down was about communication with my partner. We've been together for about a year, so we're in the early stages of learning how to talk with each other.

"When I was thinking of the movie at the beginning, a real movie came to my mind—*Silence of the Lambs*—not because it's horrible, but because that's me. I tend to shut down. When I do that, he mirrors it by shutting down, too.

"In the exercise at the end, butterflies started flying, the sun changed the image, and I felt confident that we would get through it. It feels so good to have hope that it really is going to work out."

Hopefulness is common in layer four.

I asked the group if anyone else felt better than they had at the beginning, and nearly everyone said they did. I asked how they felt in their bodies, and the replies included, "Like I could take a nap," "I feel more calm," and, "I feel less anxious." That's common in this layer, too.

If you can allow five minutes for Remembrance,
rather than five breaths,
you'll experience that much more relief.

Sometimes I spend thirty or sixty minutes with one concern or question. Other times, I practice Remembrance with an empty mind and simply enjoy the way my body and heart relax as I repeat the name of God that feels best to me. There is no wrong way to do Remembrance.

You can do Remembrance silently, anywhere, at any time.
Even during a business meeting.

Any time that you spend in Remembrance will be supportive. The information you receive will be different each time because it will depend on your concern or question. But the way that your body responds, the way your heart responds, those will be similar; this is the nature of it.

*Remembrance opens our hearts, bodies,
minds, and spirits to love, and it quickly transports us
from the more superficial layers to layer four.*

You don't have to be concerned about something in order to do Remembrance. You can simply enjoy that wonderful light coming toward you and the name of God or word that feels best to you. Opening to love like that can spark surprising responses in others, as I found out one sunny day in March.

Sitting on a park bench outside the historic Gruene Hall in New Braunfels, Texas, my friend and I soaked up the warm sunshine while her two boys climbed a tree nearby. Stephanie and her family had traveled from Montana to see her brother-in-law perform in "the oldest continually running dance hall in Texas," and everyone was in high spirits.

While I listened to Stephanie tell me about their visit to San Antonio, I paid attention—not only to her words, but also to the thoughts crossing my mind, my emotions, and my body sensations. I consciously relaxed my lower body and took long, slow breaths. I noticed how good it felt to have my dear friend next to me. This was a delicious day.

*I imagined my heart could open up and radiate love
toward Steph's boys, in the same way the sunshine bathed all of us,
not requiring a response, but simply offering a gift.*

Stephanie was in midsentence when both of us saw a little girl with blonde ringlets and big, blue eyes toddling toward me with her arms outstretched. I reached down to her, picked her up, said, "Well, hi there!" and kissed her fluffy cheek. The little girl laid her head on my right shoulder, and her body relaxed against mine.

I rubbed her back and began gently rocking from side to side as I quietly said to Stephanie, "Watch for someone who might be looking for her." For several minutes, the three of us were in our own world.

Watching the little girl in awe, Stephanie said, "Her eyes are half closed, and she has a dreamy look on her face." I was in heaven.

Eventually, a young woman approached us, and I stood up, expecting my little companion to stir. She didn't; she just stayed completely relaxed on my shoulder. The woman introduced herself and said my new friend was her niece, Kennedy, and she was eighteen months old.

I rubbed Kennedy's back again and gently said, "Kennedy, look who's here." She looked up but again made no movement to leave my arms. Kennedy's aunt reached out and took her, and then I caressed Kennedy's cheek and said, "Thank you," before they walked away.

I will never, ever forget that day. The whole day, my focus had been simply on feeling and radiating love. I had let go of my agenda. I had decided to completely enjoy whatever that day brought me, without trying to control anything.

When I dissolved into love, love was reflected back to me, and the day was better than I ever would have thought to create for myself. I like to remember my snuggle with Kennedy whenever

I feel worried about the future and am trying to control what happens. She is a reminder that ...

Love brings me everything I need,
and more, when I am open.

Since that day in Texas, other children have approached me in the same way. It is no longer surprising to me when a child I've never met climbs into my lap or hugs me, usually without a word. It's a wonderful gift I get to receive when I focus on receiving and radiating love, without any expectations.

Remembrance is a wondrous practice. It opens me to joy, peace, and love—eventually. Sometimes I experience comfort quickly, and other times Remembrance first opens me up to painful thoughts, physical sensations, or emotions that I've been holding onto, so they can be healed.

There is a lot of wisdom in a phrase commonly heard
in support groups: the pain is in the resistance.

If, like me, you find that physical distress, fear, sadness, or anger has accumulated for years, it might help to know that those emotions will become softer if you let them out, breathe, and let love in.

Remember the story about my tax bill and my fear that I would not have enough money? In order to get beyond my fearful reaction, I had to open to the fear and allow tears to flow. Then, there was room for reassurance and peace to come in.

Layer four helps us open to what is in our highest good.

This is wonderful news, right? Yes, it is, but I want to prepare you, because what is in our highest good doesn't always feel good. It does, however, always lead to healing.

The process I went through with my tax bill was very quick; I experienced all four layers in about three minutes. Sometimes relief comes quickly, but other times, I have to be patient with myself when I am afraid the pain will overwhelm me. In those moments, I reach out for help and take it one step at a time.

Earlier, I told you about how I was in reaction toward the manager of my first apartment in Missoula. It is true that forgiving the property manager helped me relax and let go of my anger. But it's also true that I felt very uncomfortable inside my apartment, and I wasn't sure why.

I decided to spend a week at my new home and work with a counselor by phone to see if I could figure out why the apartment bothered me so much and resolve it. At the time, I had no idea what I was getting myself into.

Each day, I had an hour-long session on the phone with a counselor named Ryhana, as well as twice-daily check-ins and assigned readings. Early on, I told Ryhana about my discomfort in the apartment and my desire to understand what was driving it. She helped me by guiding me into Remembrance, just as I have guided you.

Hearing someone guide me and knowing that they are with me really helps me open. On the second or third day, I realized what was causing my unease. The ceiling and sliding glass door in my apartment reminded me of an apartment my father had lived in when I was five years old and he was separated from my mom.

Not only was that a terrible time in my young life because of the separation and divorce, but also I experienced and witnessed very traumatic events in my dad's apartment. The realization of why my new apartment bothered me hit me like cold water to the face. For a moment, I stopped breathing. Then, I heard myself crying inside, "No! I don't want to face that!"

But I faced it anyway. I could face it because I was not alone. I had the support of Ryhana, Rebecca, and two trusted friends. And I had my own previous experience to remind me that when I turn toward my pain and open to love, whatever is causing the pain heals.

I share this story with you because I don't want you to be surprised if one day you practice Remembrance or another reflection exercise and become aware of something painful that feels really big. It's a good thing when that happens because it's a sign that the "big" thing is ready to be healed. If you have experienced trauma, please consider giving yourself the gift of professional support as you heal. I do believe it's possible to heal trauma on our own, but I would never recommend it because healing on our own takes much longer and is more painful than necessary.

My week-long retreat marked the beginning of a year-long healing journey, during which I took full advantage of trustworthy support (and lots of tissue!). I have listed the resources that helped me on my website, www.anniebwilson.com, in case they might help you as well.

Even though it took a year to heal myself from the residue of my memories, as soon as I had made the connection to my dad's former apartment and shared that with Ryhana, my reaction to my own apartment lessened. "The truth shall set you free …"

Within a couple of weeks, I was able to walk around in that space and remind myself that 1) it was 2007, not 1975; 2) I was safe; and 3) I had been drawn to live in that apartment specifically so that my painful memories could be triggered and healed. I never really liked that apartment, but I no longer felt uncomfortable there.

By the end of my year-long lease, I no longer needed to live in a space that triggered me because I had healed the trauma related to my dad's apartment. I was ready to move, and I easily found a house that matched my ideal of a nurturing home.

That same kind of relief and healing are available to you.

They might rush in quickly, or it might take time for you to gently turn toward your own pain and the love that heals it. When you are not sure what to do next, pause. Be gentle and go slowly.

Your own pace is right for you.

There are many wonderful resources and ways to approach healing. I am simply sharing with you the resources that have helped me shift from perfectionism and isolation to gentleness and love. Every microscopic shift we make toward layer four is an act of supreme courage and self-care.

Remembrance and other spiritual practices are called "practices" because it takes practice to connect to the deeper layers of communication and stay in our hearts. It is a process of self-care that, for me, opens up a whole new world of peace, hope, and positive communication. Whatever progress you make is good. It is worthy of celebration. And it is enough.

You are enough.
Right now.

An Example of Walking through the Four Layers of Communication

Let's summarize the four layers of communication by walking through them with Steven, a client of mine who struggled through limiting, painful beliefs. While I describe Steven's experience, I'll teach you another practice that can help you move through the layers, to shift from fear to hope and from constriction to openness.

Steven came to me one day feeling distraught and exhausted. He had wanted to quit his job at an investment firm for some time but believed that he couldn't unless he had a clear plan for what would happen next. That day, after many weeks of effort, he still had no idea what should come next. He knew only that he wanted out of his job and that he could not get out until he had a plan.

Every time he looked at a job in his industry, Steven's energy dropped, and he felt a sense of dread. He had put in a few applications but didn't really want them to come to anything; he just wanted something in place because he couldn't leave his job until he had a plan. Are you beginning to recognize a limiting belief Steven carried?

Beginning in Layer One

Limiting beliefs like *I have to have a plan* generate fear, which constricts us and keeps us in layer one. Remember how we think and behave in that layer? In layer one, we focus on what's wrong. When we think of ourselves, we notice only what we need to change in order to be happy. Steven was in layer one when he decided he could not have what he wanted (freedom from his current job) until he changed something else (by developing a plan for what to do next).

When he arrived in my office, I invited Steven to choose where he would like to sit. We'd had a pattern of sitting in the same places, and I thought it might help to introduce a simple, low-risk choice. I said, "I want you to remember that you can sit anywhere you'd like. We don't have to sit in the same chairs as usual."

Steven replied, "Thanks, but I like the hug chair."

The chair he referred to wraps inward, just enough so that it feels like you're being hugged when you sit in it. Steven had never called his chair the "hug chair" before, and I smiled as I said, "Great, then that's where you'll sit today."

Even though he was feeling lost,
Steven still knew what he wanted in that moment.

His choice to sit in a chair that felt like a hug was an act of self-care. It's important to notice this because someday you might not have a clue about how to make a big decision, and you might feel overcome by confusion. If you pause to ask yourself, *What do I really want in this moment?* you might realize that a small choice can bring big relief. In that moment, Steven wanted to feel the comfort of sitting in the hug chair, and as he settled into it, he let out a deep sigh.

I sat in the other hug chair, glad he had chosen those for us, and opened with, "Steven, you look so exhausted today. How are you feeling?"

Steven said, "I am totally exhausted. This morning, as I parked my car at work, I asked myself, *Do I really have to do this for one more day?* I didn't want to walk into my office, and the day was overwhelmingly busy."

Identifying Patterns

As Steven continued to share about his day, he talked about how much he wished he had a plan so he could leave that job. I asked if we could pause for a moment. Then I asked Steven why he had to have a plan. Whose voice was he listening to? Startled, Steven said, "It's my voice, of course."

I gently asked him, "Where have you heard that before?"

Who else in your life always had to have a plan?

Steven answered, "My dad. He always had a plan, and we always stuck to the plan, no matter what. He taught me that planning was the key to success."

I asked, "Would you say that your dad's plans brought you and the family happiness?"

Steven thought for a moment and then replied, "Some of the time, yes, and some of the time, no. There were times when I wished he would just relax and play with me in the yard, even though it wasn't scheduled." I invited Steven to pause and notice how his heart and body were feeling.

Moving into Layer Two

He said, "My chest feels like there's a bowling ball sitting on it." Stephen put a hand to his heart and continued, "My stomach feels tight and upset. I can sense some sadness, but it's pretty deep below the surface. I don't feel it; I just know it's there."

*In layer two, we start to notice our emotions and body sensations
but we focus on what we believe should be,
not on what our deep hearts want.*

Steven had entered layer two. He was aware of how his body felt, and he was beginning to notice how his heart felt. His thoughts were focused on what his father wanted, which is common in layer two when we focus on what we believe should be, even if it contradicts what we want for ourselves. Also, in layer two, we notice what someone else needs to change in order for us to be happy. If he wanted to stay in the pain of layer two, Steven could have focused on trying to change his father's belief that everyone should have a plan. Instead, he chose to move on toward layer three.

"Good," I said. "It's great that you can sense how your heart and body are feeling. That awareness is enough right now. There is no need to try to make anything else happen. Would you like to take a closer look at the belief that you have to have a plan, so we can see if it's really true?"

"Definitely," Steven replied.

I began to guide Steven through a process that you can use, too. It's as simple as "if/then." It's simple, but like everything I've been showing you, the results are sometimes complex, and always healing.

Exploring with If/Then

I knew that Steven followed a spiritual path and called the divine God, so I invited him to close his eyes and imagine that God was between him and everyone else. I suggested, "Imagine that God's light and love are filling the space between you and me." I paused for a moment and then said, "When that's clear, imagine that God's light and love are all around you, embracing you like the hug chair is right now. Take your time, breathe gently, and let me know when you are ready to continue."

When Steven indicated that he was ready, I asked him what would happen if he did not have a plan. I explained, "We want to identify the risk involved so that we can name the fear that's driving this belief. Try completing this sentence: if I don't have a plan, then …"

Steven said, "Then I will disappoint people."

"Okay," I replied. "And if you disappoint people, then …"

"Then they will go away—wait, I know that's not true. That's a stupid thought," Steven said as he laughed self-consciously.

Painful beliefs are not shaped by logic.
They are shaped by fear.

I then politely explained, "Your mind knows that it isn't true, but there is a part of you that does believe it. That's why it hurts. The most efficient way to change painful beliefs begins with giving them room for expression without judgment."

Relaxing into Layer Three

Steven was approaching layer three, where he would be able to recognize the core belief that was causing his pain. He was getting closer to seeing the difference between what he wanted and what his dad wanted, allowing both to be okay.

In layer three, we are able to recognize the space
between ourselves and other people
rather than seeing ourselves
bound by other people's opinions or actions.

In that moment, Steven's heart was softening even more, but his mind was still in the driver's seat. Steven was still attached to logic because he was afraid of feeling how hurtful his core belief was. That's okay. I reminded him, just as I have reminded you, that it is good to be gentle and go slowly.

"Okay." Steven sighed, took a deep breath, and then quietly said, "If I disappoint people, then … I will not please them."

"And if you do not please them, then …"

"Then they will leave me," Steven said, this time without criticizing himself.

I encouraged him to relax his belly a bit more, remember God's presence all around him, and pause for a few breaths. As he breathed in, the color came back to Steven's cheeks, and his shoulders, which had been hunched with tension, relaxed. He sighed, rubbed his hand over his heart, and nodded to let me know he was ready to continue.

Opening to Love in Layer Four

As Steven opened to divine support, he moved into layer four. The fear gave way, his mind relaxed, his heart softened, and his body and spirit opened. From this place, Steven was able to go even deeper because he had let go of his need to be right. He was open to whatever God wanted to show him.

I asked, "If people leave you, then what?"

"Then it's true that I am not enough," he said. Steven opened his eyes and exclaimed, "It all comes back to enoughness, doesn't it? That's amazing!"

We both laughed, enjoying the release of energy, and I said, "Yes, it always comes back to enoughness, for all of us. Would you like to check out the truthfulness of that last statement?"

"Absolutely!" Steven replied. He had done this before, so he knew his heart would feel much better in just a moment.

Perceiving Truth in Remembrance

Steven began to practice Remembrance. He adjusted a bit in his hug chair to allow one foot to rest on the ground, closed his eyes, and softly repeated the name of God that felt best to him. After about eight to ten gentle repetitions of God's name, Steven asked, "Is it true that I am not enough?"

I could tell he was receiving a loving response because I watched as tears slowly made their way down Steven's cheeks. I asked Steven what he was noticing, and he said, "I just saw an image of my father. He looked at me so lovingly, and with a soft smile, he said, 'My beloved son, you are enough, just as you are.'" With that, Steven started sobbing.

I said to him, "That's good, Steven. There is no need to change anything. We have plenty of time."

Years of pent-up sadness and fear released as Steven allowed his tears to flow, without shame, without judgment. When he was ready, Steven opened his eyes, and we sat in silence together. Eventually, he said, "I feel so tired. But now it feels like a good tired."

When we move into layer four and check out the truthfulness of our painful beliefs, a lot of energy can move.

"That's what just happened for you," I explained. "The belief that you must have a plan in order to be enough takes a lot of energy to sustain. Now, your body, heart, and spirit are letting you know just how hard they've been working to help you live under the weight of that belief. Rest and lots of water will help."

*If you practice Remembrance, the next time that
painful belief, "I am not enough," sneaks in,
it will be easier because you have created an excellent foundation.*

"You are opening to the truth that you are enough right now. How does that feel?"

"Like a huge relief," Steven said, and a big smile came to his lips as he closed his eyes and sank further into his hug chair.

A few weeks later, Steven told me that he had given notice of his resignation to his employer. His face glowed when he told me, "I do feel a little fearful, not knowing what's going to happen. But mostly I feel excited and so, so relieved."

Treating the Roots

Steven and I could have spent our time seeing if it was true that he had to have a plan before leaving his job. That would have been fine, and he probably would have made some progress. I guided him toward identifying *why* he believed he had to have a plan because I knew that if he challenged the core belief, *I am not enough,* everything else would change naturally.

It's as if there were a tree whose leaves were withering from an unknown disease. We could treat each leaf individually, figuring out what was harming it and doing what we could to make it well. That might work, but it would take a lot of energy, wouldn't it? Instead, we could treat the roots of the tree and allow it to deliver the medicine to every leaf. That's what we are doing when we ask, *Is it true that I am not enough?*

*When we identify painful core beliefs and hold them up to the light,
all the painful statements stemming from them heal, too.*

Concluding Thoughts

Remember, it all comes down to enoughness, for all of us. Every time you open to the truth that you are enough, right now, you make it easier to experience what you really want, in any circumstance and any relationship. Healthy communication is your birthright, for it is an expression of the love that is you.

Afterword: *Self-Care in Communication*

"If you are not suffering,
you must be doing something *right*."
-John Wadude Laird, MD

For much of my life, I believed that suffering was a sign that I was doing something right. I thought that unless I was suffering, I wasn't working hard enough. If I actually liked my job, I thought it was a sign of laziness or that I wasn't being challenged enough. Thank goodness I now understand that *not* suffering is good. I have learned to care for myself.

Throughout the previous chapters, I have touched on the importance of self-care, but I think it warrants a chapter of its own. Your on-going progress toward healthy communication relies on how well you care for yourself. You have the tools now to shift negative or limiting core beliefs about yourself, which is a sacred act of self-care. In this chapter, I'll describe three simple yet powerful acts of self-care, as well as some tips you can use to develop the worthy habit of treating yourself kindly.

Receive What You Crave

In order to benefit from kindness, love, or compassion offered by someone else, we must open to receive it. Remember the story about my classmate in graduate school? Even though she was being offered compassion by the faculty, she was not fully receiving it.

Sure, she took advantage of the second chances they gave her, but she stayed attached to her perception that life was unfair. She did not take in the compassion that was offered deeply enough to shift her perception.

The number-one best way to start caring for yourself is to open up to the good that already surrounds you.

You don't have to do anything to earn the goodness; it already is with you. For example, there have been times when I felt incredibly lonely but was able to feel some relief when I decided to look for signs that I was not alone.

As soon as I made that decision, I started to notice strangers smiling at me, children playing near me, clients expressing gratitude for our work together. These forms of communication had been expressed all along but had escaped my notice because I was distracted by my loneliness and my belief that I had to do more in order to become worthy of the love and fellowship I craved.

*By shifting my attention, I opened to receive
what already was available to me,
and I felt less alone.*

One rainy Friday afternoon, a friend came to me feeling overwhelmed by the stress of her job and the recent loss of her beloved uncle. She asked for my advice regarding an employee whose attitude was very challenging; my friend thought it needed to be addressed immediately.

I told her I understood why she would want to speak to this employee right away, but then I invited her to pause for a moment and take a breath. I asked her how she was feeling about her uncle.

Tears immediately came to her eyes, and she said, "I can't think about that right now."

I replied, "I know you don't want to go into the feelings right now, and that's okay. I just asked the question to help you acknowledge that your heart is in pain. How long did you say your employee has had an attitude problem? Six years? Another few days is not going to make the difference between whether or not she changes. But, if you wait and give your attention to what you need, I think you'll find it much easier to talk to her in a productive way." She quietly let out a sigh of relief.

I then encouraged my friend to notice every time her children or her husband showed her that they loved her. She knew in her mind that they loved her, but her heart needed to be reminded.

Her pace had gotten so sped up by the crises around her that she had become disconnected from her heart.

As a result, she felt irritated with herself, her employees, and her family. When I made that suggestion, the tears started flowing. I said, "The reason the tears are coming is that your heart so deeply wants to know that you are supported and loved. Isn't that right?"

She nodded.

"You have always been the one to take care of everything. This is your chance to allow help to come to you. It's already being offered, but you have to open to receive it. Can you do that tonight?" Again, she nodded. We hugged and she went on her way.

The following Monday, she met with her employee and told me that the discussion had gone very well. She was glad that she had waited and had spent the weekend enjoying each moment with her kids and her husband. She had received the support she so deeply needed.

It is important to notice that my friend did nothing to change the way her family acted toward her. She did not need to convince them to love her or offer their support. They wanted to support her and were delighted that she finally let them.

Embrace Gentleness and Rest

The second most important elements of self-care are gentleness and rest. While I was writing this book, I also was working full-time as the director of organizational development for a regional hospital, coaching private clients, giving workshops, and settling into a new home.

Often, I would flop into bed exhausted but find that I couldn't rest because my mind was so full of ideas for the book. This was a good problem to have, of course, but eventually I became pretty worn out.

One Saturday morning, I awoke with my mind racing. All my body wanted to do was sleep, but instead I lay there trying to decide what to tackle first: laundry, house cleaning, book writing, grocery shopping—you get the idea.

Rather than "shoulding" all over myself as I used to do, I paused and asked for guidance. I asked, "Please help me to know what is the next right thing for me to do."

Three hours later, I was awakened by a friend's phone call. That's when I realized that the right thing for me had been to rest, just as my body had told me.

Asking for guidance is a form of gentleness.
It helps us say yes to what we already know.

Even though I know that it's okay for me to listen to my body or heart when my mind is shouting, sometimes it's difficult for me to do because some habits are resilient. I was extremely hard on myself for decades. Sometimes I need an extra helping of gentleness to overcome the "shoulds."

In those moments when my anxiety is up and my mind is filled with reasons why I shouldn't rest, if I pause and ask for guidance, what comes to my awareness is always gentle and loving. When I follow that guidance, I feel much better, I have more energy for my to-do lists, and my attention is drawn to gratitude instead of weariness.

Dwell in Gratitude

Gratitude expands the realm of what is possible in this moment. In the summer of 1998, I worked as a trainer and front-desk manager in Yellowstone National Park. My staff had come to the park to hike, make new friends, and enjoy their summer. They had not expected to be yelled at on a daily basis by weary travelers, but that's what happened.

I didn't have a budget for activities that might increase employee satisfaction, so I had to get creative. I decided to do an experiment with gratitude by creating what I called the Good News Log.

At the beginning of their shift, each employee was required to read and initial another log called the Front Desk Log. This log was our way of passing on information related to room maintenance, guest requests, and other hotel business. I hung the Good News Log right next to the Front Desk Log and communicated three guidelines:

1. Anyone from any department could write in or read the Good News Log.
2. No one was required to read the log or to write in it.
3. Anything could be written in the log, as long as it was good news.

This experiment turned into a hot topic of conversation in other departments, as well as my own. One of my employees wrote that he had checked his third-grade teacher into the hotel. Another wrote about singing beside a campfire with Bette Midler. It became common for employees to write appreciative notes to one another, too. The Good News Log became a source of encouragement and inspiration.

It helped all of us to remember that even though working at the front desk could be difficult, there was a lot to be grateful for and to celebrate. In fact, one of my night clerks told me it was the only reason she hadn't quit. The log helped her feel connected to her coworkers and included in the conversation.

*Gratitude is such an important part of self-care
because it transforms our perspective.*

Even though my employees were being yelled at by angry guests, they were able to stay grounded in the good that was happening all around them. By practicing gratitude, they reminded themselves that life was full of fun surprises, even when it also was full of challenges.

Dare to Dream

I hope you will take a moment to think about how you would like to take care of yourself. Can you open up to your yearning for ease or joy and put it into words? Do you notice your body sensations, thoughts, or emotions responding to this invitation? Pretend you are an explorer navigating a beautiful, forgotten landscape and …

Just for this moment,
pretend that anything is possible.

If anything were possible, what would you like to experience? What would you like to do for yourself? How would you like to feel? What creative activities would you like to try? Take a few minutes to write down everything that comes to your mind. Don't stop to correct your spelling or censor yourself; just let it flow. Do your best to notice what happens in your heart and body as you write.

Since our minds don't know the difference,
we reap lots of benefits from pausing to make room for our dreams,
even if five minutes later we have to take out the trash.

Guess what? If you did that activity, you just completed an act of self-care. Even though we all have responsibilities and limited budgets, we can imagine our ideal experience. Think of my staff in Yellowstone. When they reminded themselves of the ways in which their summer matched their expectations, they felt happier, and the hard stuff became much easier to deal with.

Consider setting aside time each month to read and add to what you've written. Notice how you feel when you look at your writing. If you feel inspired, really dive into that inspiration. Let it fill you up until you are so full, you can't take any more!

If you feel sad when you look at it, take that as a sign that a painful belief is hanging around. Experiment with the tips and exercises in each layer of communication, and see what you discover about yourself as you challenge that painful belief. You might find that your dreams really are within your reach. Eventually, you will open to the truth …

You are worthy of every one of them.

Tips for Self-Care

RECOGNIZE WHEN YOU ARE IN REACTION.
Know that *you* are in reaction, and take responsibility for your reaction. Then pause, pause, and pause some more.

This might seem like overkill, but really, pausing and moving out of reaction are essential acts of self-care. It is possible for us to notice our emotions, body sensations, intuition, and deeper thoughts only after we have moved through reaction. Otherwise, we will just continue to survive, living in a state of high alert, waiting for threat to appear.

ASK YOURSELF, *WHAT IS THIS REALLY ABOUT?* AND NOTICE THE FIRST THING THAT COMES TO YOUR MIND.
This is a very effective way to access your intuition. The first thing that occurs to you after you ask the question will be from your spirit/intuition. Anything after that will be from your mind, which might be helpful or it might be confusing. When you can, give your full attention to the first thing that comes to you.

SLOW EVERYTHING DOWN.

Do one thing at a time. When eating, take smaller bites and chew each one until it is liquefied. Notice how the food tastes and how it feels in your mouth. Drive for ten minutes without talking on the phone or listening to the radio.

Sometimes, slowing down can inspire anxiety. If that happens to you, do your best to allow yourself to be curious about what is behind the anxiety. You'll probably find a painful belief just waiting to be healed with love.

REMEMBER: WHEN YOU ARE UPSET, IT REALLY ISN'T ABOUT ANOTHER PERSON OR EVENT.

It is about something deeper within yourself, usually a fear or painful belief about yourself.

One very nurturing act of self-care is to remind yourself that you have the power to respond to what you need. You might pause and ask yourself, *What do I need in this moment?* Or, *How am I feeling right now?* Then notice the first thing that occurs to you.

PRACTICE RECEIVING.

If you don't recognize opportunities to receive, it might be time for you to ask for help or challenge the belief that you have to do everything. Receiving can be as simple as opening up to share a smile with a stranger.

PRACTICE GRATITUDE.

It can be powerful and fun to keep a gratitude journal. Make a commitment to write at least one thing in your gratitude journal every day for a week. At the end of the week, notice how your energy and general outlook have changed.

TRUST YOUR BODY.

Your body is designed to release the energy of stress and trauma. All you need to do is allow your body to do what it spontaneously wants to do (laugh, cry, tremble, blink rapidly, sleep, run, play, etc.).

BREATHE FULLY.

Deep breathing relaxes the survival response and stimulates the release of endorphins throughout your body. Spending two minutes breathing fully every hour during the workday can ward off late-afternoon weariness.

SHARE EYE CONTACT WITH SOMEONE.

Eye contact is so powerful because when we look into someone's eyes, our brains release a hormone called oxytocin. Oxytocin, nicknamed the "love drug," supports bonding between newborns and mothers. It also has been found to increase adults' sense of social connection and to decrease anxiety and fear.[13]

If you don't have a person you want to share eye contact with, you can gaze into your dog or cat's eyes—studies have shown that this increases our oxytocin levels, too.[14] I've even tried it on myself! After I get past the initial goofiness of it, looking into my own eyes in a mirror can be a pretty powerful experience.

LOOK OUT THE WINDOW OR STEP OUTSIDE.

Give your full attention to what your senses perceive when you look out the window or step outside. This can refresh and clear your mind and help you to remember that there is much more to life than work.

Maintain a nurturing spiritual practice.

Some people feel spiritually nurtured in the woods, and for others it's while doing yoga, attending church, meditating, or taking long baths. Your spirit is where your deeper self resides; experiment with different activities to find the ones that support you.

Celebrate progress.

Treat yourself with the same care as you would treat a baby taking his first step. Would you criticize that baby for hesitating or falling down? Or would you applaud every movement that brought him closer to his goal? Celebrating progress generates the energy we need to continue growing.

Keep your dreams alive!

You are worthy of every one of them.

Acknowledgments

Follow a pathway that is true.
Stay on it and your future
will be more wonderful
than you can possibly imagine
at this moment.
~Oscar G. Mink

The depth of my gratitude to those who have helped me to heal and to know my true, playful, holy self cannot be expressed; tears come to my eyes when I think of how lovingly and faithfully they have guided me through the terrain of my own being. Rebecca Halima, thank you for walking through your healing journey and in the process becoming ever more well prepared to guide others like me through our own. Thank you for meeting me wherever and in whatever state I am, wrapping me in Love and helping me to witness Truth inside myself.

Thank you, Oscar, for not allowing me to hide behind your coattails and for demonstrating the appropriateness of speaking of love in all places, even boardrooms. I miss you. Thank you, Doug, for being my champion, my beloved, my best friend and partner in all things. Your love opens me to Life. Thank you, Brad and Ed, for helping me to relearn what it feels like to be in my own body and to listen to my body's voice. Stephanie A'amina, my soul sister, thank you for engaging with me in a friendship that sheds light onto the scariest of places, celebrates every child's perfection, and wraps life in a warm embrace. And to my clients and readers, thank you for allowing me the privilege of coming alongside of you and joining your journey toward remembering that you are enough, just as you are.

Notes

1. Brent Davis, Dennis Sumara, and Rebecca Luce-Kapler, *Engaging Minds: Learning and Teaching in a Complex World* (Mahway, NJ: Lawrence Erlbaum Associates, 2000).

2. Thomas Lewis, MD, Fari Amini, MD, and Richard Lannon, MD, *A General Theory of Love* (New York, NY: Vintage Books, 2000).

3. Cynthia M. Perkins, Ed., "Dysautonomia—Autonomic Nervous System Dysfunction," Holistichelp.net. http://www.holistichelp.net/dysautonomia-autonomic-nervous-system-dysfunction.html (retrieved June 11, 2012).

4. Stephen Buhner, "The Heart as an Organ of Perception," *Spirituality & Health* (March–April 2006): 36.

5. Chris Mercogliano and Kim Debus, "Expressing Life's Wisdom: Nurturing Heart-Brain Development Starting with Infants," *Journal of Family Life* 5 (1999): 1.

6. Barbara Ann Brennan, *Hands of Light: A Guide to Healing Through the Human Energy Field* (New York, NY: Bantam Books, 1987).

7. Thayer and Smith, "Greek Lexicon entry for Aphesis," *The New Testament Greek Lexicon*, http://www.studylight.org/lex/grk/view.cgi?number=859 (retrieved June 11, 2012).

8. Davis et al. 2000.

9. J. Luiselli and D. Reed, *Behavioral Sport Psychology: Evidence-Based Approaches to Performance* (New York, NY: Springer, 2011).

10. Peter Levine, *Waking the Tiger: Healing Trauma* (Berkeley, CA: North Atlantic Books, 1997).

11. Elisabeth Sifton, *The Serenity Prayer: Faith and Politics in Times of Peace and War* (New York, NY: W.W. Norton & Co., Inc., 2003).

12. Sidi Shaykh Muhammad al-Jamal ar-Rifa'I as-Shadhuli, *Music of the Soul: Sufi Teachings* (Petaluma, CA: Sidi Muhammad Press, 1994).

13. K. Macdonald and T. M. Macdonald, "The Peptide that Binds: A Systemic Review of Oxytocin and Its Prosocial Effects in Humans," *Harvard Review of Psychiatry* 18, no. 1 (2010): 1–21.

14. M. Nagasawa, T. Kikusui, T. Onaka, and M. Ohta, "Dog's Gaze at Its Owner Increases Owner's Urinary Oxytocin During Social Interaction," *Hormones and Behavior* 55, no. 3 (2009): 434–441.

Annie Barron Wilson, Ph.D., is the first communication expert to explain how we can transform conflict into connection by engaging the mind, body, heart and spirit. She radiates a beautiful balance of strength and sensitivity required to move and touch people's lives in the deepest way. Annie is an award winning author and recognized expert in communication and conflict resolution. Her personal mission is to increase hope and transform communication by helping people remember they are valuable and powerful. In addition to more than 20 years experience as a manager, business owner, speaker and coach, Annie holds degrees from The University of Texas at Austin, Cornell University and University of Oregon. Dr. Wilson brings to her work insight gained through decades of her own spiritual and emotional healing, which is one reason why her clients experience profound results quickly. She lives in Austin, Texas with her beloved, Doug Wilson. For more information, please visit www.anniebwilson. com.

www.ingramcontent.com/pod-product-compliance
Lightning Source LLC
Chambersburg PA
CBHW020419290526
45785CB00002B/635